WILD ROSES ARE WORTH IT

KEVIN VAN TIGHEM

WILD ROSES ARE WORTH IT

REIMAGINING THE
ALBERTA ADVANTAGE

RMB

For information on purchasing bulk quantities of this book, or to obtain media excerpts or invite the author to speak at an event, please visit rmbooks.com and select the "Contact" tab.

RMB | Rocky Mountain Books Ltd.
rmbooks.com
@rmbooks
facebook.com/rmbooks

Cataloguing data available from Library and Archives Canada
ISBN 9781771604857 (softcover)
ISBN 9781771604864 (electronic)

Cover photo: iStock.com/Prostock-Studio

Printed and bound in Canada

We acknowledge the financial support of the Government of Canada through the Canada Book Fund and the Canada Council for the Arts, and of the province of British Columbia through the British Columbia Arts Council and the Book Publishing Tax Credit.

Disclaimer
The views expressed in this book are those of the author and do not necessarily reflect those of the publishing company, its staff, or its affiliates.

CONTENTS

3 THE COST OF OIL

4 AGRICULTURE

5 PARKS

6 WILD MEAT

7 BEING BETTER

FOREWORD

In the summer of 2007 I criss-crossed the prairies and Rockies in a marshmallow-shaped five-ton selling books to small-town stores and gift shops. The most interesting title on my publisher's backlist was *Home Range: Writings on Conservation and Restoration*, by Kevin Van Tighem. The writing gave deeper meaning to the landscapes I was driving through – urban, farm and wilderness alike. It was the only book I kept in the truck's cab, and in my down time I read it from cover to cover.

Four and a half years later I was editing *Alberta Views* magazine when a pitch arrived in my inbox from the same Kevin Van Tighem. He proposed to write a reflection on Banff National Park, where he'd just retired as superintendent (after working across the national parks system for three decades). Of course I said yes. The subsequent story, "Silence in the Park," contrasted hikes Kevin took 35 years apart on what was once the Cascade fire road. It showed how good decision making (e.g., the closure of said fire road) has gradually discouraged harmful human visitation in the park, but also how climate change is altering Banff's wilderness more profoundly than humans ever have before.

Kevin would write another story for AV, then another, and he kept pitching more – on headwaters, land conservation, aquifers, the reintroduction of bison to Banff, the legacy of Charlie Russell, coal strip mining, grass-fed beef. I couldn't say no. I was learning too much from Kevin. I enjoyed his observing and questioning and how he expressed both in writing. AV readers called in to ask for more such articles. His stories won awards. Best of all, I really enjoyed talking with Kevin about his drafts, my edits, his revisions, the fact-checking process and his ideas for still more stories.

I finally asked him in late 2013 if – in addition to writing long-form pieces for AV – he would contribute a regular column. He agreed and proposed the name "This Land," as "most of what I write is around better understanding of where we live and what living here entails by way of good decisions." It's the perfect name for his column. "This Land" not only speaks to Kevin's overarching passion but evokes the 1940 Woody Guthrie song, which is best known as a celebration of good stewardship but is also a protest anthem decrying private property, where individuals' decisions about land, for better or for worse, affect all of us.

The name also speaks to me pointedly about place. *This* land. Not the rainforest in Brazil, whose violations Albertans can do nothing about. Not the polluted rivers of China, or America's famous superfund sites (the Love Canal, the Berkeley Pit), which we often know better than our own messes. *This* land is *our* land – these mountains and foothills and prairies and boreal forest and rivers – along with these oil sands tailings ponds and gravel pits and sprawling suburbs. As citizens of a democracy we're not only able to influence the decisions made about this land on our behalf, we have a responsibility to do so. Reading Kevin inspires me to hold my government to account.

Through his writing Kevin demonstrates the eye for detail and arcane knowledge of a plant ecologist, the authority of a deeply informed critic, the wary pragmatism of someone who knows too well the workings of bureaucracy, the lived experience and love for the land of a fourth-generation Albertan, the soul of a poet. From conversations with AV readers I know that Kevin connects with environmentalists, responsible hunters, ranchers, city slickers, conservatives, NDPers and Greens alike. (He's rather less popular with the off-road vehicle crowd.)

What's more, he can express his perspective to radio listeners or to a live audience as eloquently as he can in writing – even as he usually prefers the company of a nice cutthroat trout. To borrow a more famous magazine's motto, Kevin is a man "of no party or clique."

I've now been editing Kevin's writing for almost ten years and reading it for even longer. Over that time I've come to know Kevin as a friend. We've had many good conversations over beers. He taught my eldest daughter how to squeeze dogwood berries so that the juice squirts into her dad's eyes. He even took this reformed vegetarian on a hunt in the Whaleback, taking care to provide me with what I was assured is the first-timer's customary fluorescent orange "Elkaholic" cap. We troubled no animals that weekend. But it was, and remains, a great privilege to experience the land with Kevin as one's interpreter and guide.

—EVAN OSENTON, MAY 2020

INTRODUCTION

Wild roses bloom in June, a season of wild hopes. It's when couples traditionally wed, their eyes full of one another and their hearts filled with dreams they are determined will come true. Sometimes those dreams do. Sometimes they don't. Sometimes they find better dreams, or at least different ones.

For the first half of my life, Alberta cars sported licence plates proclaiming this to be "Wild Rose Country." It is that; the soft perfume of springtime roses rises from the edges of gravel roads carved through the northern boreal forest, the bighorn sheep slopes of the Front Ranges and the sun-bleached plains south of Medicine Hat. Not all the same kind of rose – the deep pink *Rosa woodsii* of the northern forest grows into a spindly tall shrub, while the larger *Rosa arkansana* of the prairies hides flat amid the grasses. Sometimes those prairie roses are pure white. Sometimes they are white streaked with pink, and other times they are the purest of soft pinks. Dense tangles of *Rosa acicularis* line prairie coulees and border aspen groves in the foothills, the laneways into farmsteads and the edges of urban trails. Clay-coloured sparrows perch amid the blossoms and sing their hearts out.

In 1930, after canvassing Alberta's school children, the provincial legislature declared *Rosa acicularis* the provincial flower. It was a popular choice; everybody knows those pink petals, that subtle perfume, the sight of red rosehips against winter snow. Everybody has pulled thorny twigs out of wool socks or had to wait for rose prickles to fester out of sore thumbs. These are things all Albertans know and share.

That's how the wild rose ended up on our licence plates. Then politics intervened: an upstart provincial party of the sort that sprout regularly in this province decided to call itself the Wild Rose Party. The ruling Progressive Conservatives weren't thrilled with the idea of providing their new adversaries with free advertising on the back of every car, so they did away with the slogan. They should have been patient; like others before it the Wild Rose Party bloomed briefly and died, ironically taking the Progressive Conservatives down with them. Too late: our licence plates no longer remind us who we are.

It's still Wild Rose Country, regardless, but certainly

not the same one that it was in 1930. We were a poor province in those days, and about to get poorer. The Dirty Thirties wreaked havoc on the agricultural sector, at that time the biggest part of the province's economy. Fields that had been living prairie only a half-century ago, that should never have been plowed, blew away. The dust storms darkened skies all across the prairie provinces. Farm families abandoned their homes and moved to grimy young towns and cities to make do on federal welfare and contemplate the end of all dreams. Then came a war, and all the young men went overseas – my own dad among them. It was hard to imagine a future that could work.

But those who came home found the wild roses still in bloom, and dreams waiting to be rekindled. Many fell in love, and married in June.

And so we got a baby boom, of which I am a product. And, fortuitously, not only did agriculture become prosperous again in the 1950s but speculators and entrepreneurs got lucky. They found oil. And having found oil they looked for more. They found it too. Soon there were more rose-lined gravel roads winding into the hinterland, connecting oil and gas wells, pipelines and pumping stations, and distant refineries. Roses might grow in Alberta ditches, but now money grew on trees.

It's probably safe to say that no generation was ever so richly blessed as mine. We were born into the finest place on Earth at the beginning of one of the most prosperous eras this place had ever known. Energy development was slow at first because capital, labour and technology were all in limited supply, but by the time I entered university those problems were solved and the province was transforming rapidly. One after another, from Shell Waterton to Rainbow Lake to Pembina, oil companies found lucrative new fields of pressurized hydrocarbons. The oil and gas were easy and inexpensive to extract, and the world wanted them because cheap energy created a standard of living to which nearly everyone aspired.

It helped that there was a lot more everyone. Alberta had barely a million souls when I was born; now it has well over four million. The world population has increased from 2.5 billion to almost eight billion in the same span. More transportation, more consumption, more ambitious dreams – and all driven by the stuff lying hidden in the ground beneath this place called Alberta.

When a province contains vast amounts of an energy source that fuels prosperity and is in demand by a growing global population, that province can get very wealthy. And we did. But it couldn't last. The most easily accessible and, consequently, cheapest oil and gas to produce was soon depleted. Increasingly, profit margins fell as the cost of production from deeper and more complex reserves went up. Meanwhile, other parts of the world were doing all they could to find their own oil and gas deposits and profit from them too. In the Middle East, vast shallow fields of oil have yet to be depleted. The US, by far the major market for Alberta hydrocarbons, surprised even itself in the early 21st century by becoming a net exporter of oil. All this added up to repeated price shocks that jolted the Alberta oil patch, driving down profits. As the costs of production grew, companies chose to reduce costs by replacing workers with technology; even if conventional oil hadn't been dying, the once-abundant oil jobs weren't going to last.

Climate change was an even more profound challenge. Oil, gas and coal are actually atmospheric carbon that was captured by plants over countless millions of years and stored safely away in marine sediments and ancient bogs that, buried, became embedded in rock. Extracting all that stored carbon and burning it for fuel puts it back into the atmosphere, where it becomes like glass on a greenhouse – letting radiant sunlight through but, when that sunlight turns to heat, not letting it back out. The planet is warming rapidly and that's wreaking havoc on our climates. We used to hear about climate change; now, as the consequences become increasingly evident, we talk about a climate crisis. Unprecedentedly violent storms, forest fires, floods, vanishing glaciers, eroding coastlines, melting permafrost, failed crops – the costs are mounting rapidly. All over the world people are racing to find ways to replace hydrocarbon fuels with renewable ones. With each degree of success, yet another nail goes into the coffin of the old oil and gas economies.

Still, oil and gas are hard to beat as sources of concentrated, reliable energy. That energy has enabled human populations to grow dense and wealthy in many regions, well above the natural capacity of the planet to sustain them. Many people live in urban bubbles where it seems like nature is no longer relevant; we can make anything we need now by exploiting energy more creatively. But we are, illusions of progress notwithstanding, still a part of nature. And nature has a way of dealing with populations that exceed their carrying capacity.

Disease, for example. Just as sloughs overcrowded with waterfowl become hotbeds of botulism and avian cholera, or game farms full of elk get infected with tuberculosis and chronic wasting disease, a world full of crowded cities connected by oil-fuelled transportation networks is a breeding ground just waiting for the right pestilence to arise. In 2020 that's what happened, when a coronavirus jumped from its wildlife hosts into a human population that had no immunity to it. As the world shut down its transportation networks, and then its factories and schools, and then even its neighbourhoods to try and stop the spread of the virus, the burning of fossil fuels also declined.

For Wild Rose Country's human economy, then, the second decade of the 21st century was almost the perfect storm. Alberta had become so smug and complacent, so certain that we were a chosen people for whom oil-soaked prosperity was a birthright and a guarantee, that we had no fallback plan when the rug got pulled out from under us. We are in a time as fraught as 1930, when kids, unaware of crashing stock markets and looming farm disasters, happily chose a flower for the home province they thought they knew so well.

Wild roses still bloom here each spring. But they symbolize something different now than they did in 1930, and certainly than they did during our half-century of prosperity and excess. What exactly *is* Wild Rose Country, now, at another time of disruption and change?

I never was all that fond of the oil era. I didn't like what the fevered pursuit of energy riches did to the good country into which I was born – the unreclaimed seismic lines, roads cutting deep into once pristine valleys, the stench of sour gas and the gas flares that reddened the night sky for half my life. I didn't like how the lure of oil money made kids drop out of high school and hurry off to the oil camps to make it big, giving up on the acquisition of knowledge and absorbing, instead, the prejudices of their mostly male coworkers. I didn't like those big muscle trucks, off-highway vehicles and monster boats, or the brash, entitled culture that increasingly took over from the more humble and community-centred values of the grownups I'd known in my youth. It was all the other things about Alberta that I liked – things that unfortunately tend to get crowded out by oil and the greed it inspires.

In fairness, though, I profited from it. Oil revenues built the human infrastructure that made things possible for my generation – the schools, the roads, the trails and the parks. And that's a conundrum; as an Alberta baby boomer, I'm the product of privilege no matter how much I might prefer to disdain it. It's a difficult tension that can make it hard to hold firm opinions. But I do.

I started writing in the late 1970s, mostly accounts of

hunting and fishing trips for hook-and-bullet magazines. They were about this place, and living in it deeply. They were essentially different versions of the same love story. Later, no longer content with simple storytelling, I tried my hand at investigative journalism, reflective essays and conservation polemics. Then, in 1998, a new magazine appeared on Alberta newsstands that filled a gap for many of us. It was Jackie Flanagan's labour of love: *Alberta Views*. Jackie says she launched the magazine to counter stereotypes about Alberta – that this is a place of rednecks in big trucks spending oil money on toys and sneering at everyone else in the country. Instead, her new magazine dealt with questions of social justice, environment, the arts and letters, progressive thought and critical analysis. It was a magazine that reminded us all that we still have wild roses, and that their sweet and subtle nectar can overwhelm and outlast even the strongest of diesel fumes.

Alberta Views gave me the chance to write about things that I believe make Alberta what it is. Things that aren't just about oil and money. Things worthy of deeper consideration.

This book is a collection of columns and articles originally published in that remarkable magazine. They were written to celebrate, to challenge and to reinterpret the province of my birth and what it means to be of this place. Most were written in the heady days of an oil boom that too many believed would last forever. They were meant to provide a counter-narrative to those who see this place simply as Oil-berta. But now, coming out of an oil crash and pandemic into the dust clouds of what will almost certainly be our own generation's Dirty Thirties, perhaps they offer something more. Perhaps they can help to remind us of where we actually are and, through that, help us to imagine who we will choose to be next. This is an era of unavoidable and dramatic change; we shouldn't waste time on what didn't work or what can't last. Our future won't forgive us for that, any more than it will forgive us for ruining the place for lack of care and attention to its most lasting values.

Wild roses can be difficult. They grow tangled and they are full of bristles. But they are always beautiful, when we take the time to consider them. And this is Wild Rose Country.

Whatever we choose that to mean.

It would be inappropriate to leave it at that. Some thanks are due.

I would like especially to thank Jackie Flanagan, founder and owner of *Alberta Views*, for having had the vision and perseverance to make that fine magazine a part of all our lives – helping us to consider our better selves and to imagine our best possibilities. This province, in my opinion, is a better place for the mirror she provides us and the forum she has created for voices like mine and so many other Alberta writers. Beth Ed, Miranda Foggo, Beate Wichmann, Joe Wilderson, Tadzio Richards and others of the *Alberta Views* family: I thank you all for being part of my community.

And Evan Osenton, my long-suffering editor, whose gentle touch polishes the glow into each piece I write: thanks for both your talent and your friendship.

This book is dedicated to Alberta – this land, these waters, those living creatures and the people who call it home. It's more than just our address. We *are* this place; this place is us.

1

NATURE

CRANES ON HIGH

Calm September days can feel almost surreal in central Alberta. A sleepy stillness lies over the aspen groves and prairies with the growing season past. Time seems suspended. That breathless autumn beauty surrounded me the first time I saw a crane. I was alone in the near-wilderness of the 600-km^2 Canadian Forces training base south of Wainwright. I had gone there to hunt grouse.

CFB Wainwright first opened to strictly controlled hunting for deer in the winter of 1966/67. Just turned 14, I accompanied by dad, uncle and older brother on that initial hunt and, on opening day, shot my first deer there. Several years later, the military opened the reserve to an early-autumn season for ruffed and sharp-tailed grouse. Footloose and free after having graduated from university, I decided to make a solo trip to what had become a sort of central Alberta mecca for my family.

Standing at the edge of an aspen grove, I heard a guttural, eerie croak somewhere above me in the endless blue of a perfect sky: almost certainly a bird, but one I didn't recognize in spite of years of bird study. There was a wild and unknowable quality to that sound. It seemed to speak of everything I yearned to know of far places and untamed nature.

Fishing out my binoculars, I eventually spotted them. Pale grey, wings outstretched, a column of 30 or so sandhill cranes was circling slowly in a thermal, soaring ever higher like hawks. Only they weren't hawks – they were a graceful-necked, muskeg-dwelling bird I'd long dreamed of seeing. They spiralled higher and higher; then they were gone. Later, I learned that cranes soar on thermals to conserve energy while migrating to their winter homes in the southern US and northern Mexico.

Those were lesser sandhill cranes. They had nested in the taiga and tundra of northern Canada. Years later I finally met the greater sandhill that, ironically, nests in the Alberta foothills near where, when I was a young birder, my interest in cranes first awakened.

Recently, I found my nature scrapbooks from the late 1960s. I suspect most birders are a bit obsessive-compulsive; those scrapbooks certainly offer convincing evidence. Among the newspaper clippings carefully glued into the scrapbooks was one stating that the world's population of whooping cranes – the much larger relative of the sandhill – had increased to 18.

Eighteen! I despaired of ever seeing one. Those whooping cranes all nested in Alberta, but only in remote Wood Buffalo National Park. Like the sandhills, their migration route lay far from my home; mostly in Saskatchewan. And I knew all 18 would be gone before I grew up.

More than ten times that many whooping cranes will migrate south from Wood Buffalo this fall. Breeding and reserve programs maintain other small flocks; the world population has increased to almost 300. They are almost out of danger; what a success!

I was wrong – both about their inevitable fate and about ever seeing one. For a couple years I worked in Saskatchewan's Prince Albert National Park. My wife and I decided we should take advantage of our exile from Alberta to look for whooping cranes. A bit of internet sleuthing revealed that fall migration sightings are commonest northeast of Saskatoon in mid-October.

One drizzly day we headed south through what felt like endless fields and forests. It was like searching for a needle in a haystack. But then, south of Blaine Lake, I found myself veering onto the shoulder and staring in disbelief at two white spots a kilometre away at the edge of a stubble field. Could it be?

Down a side road we found a vantage point only a

couple of hundred metres away. Two tall, elegant, adult whooping cranes were foraging along the edge of a field, accompanied by a reddish fledgling, itself larger than a sandhill crane.

Shortly after, a pickup truck pulled up with two stocky young men in it. They were keeping an eye on the cranes and making sure we didn't disturb them. The farmers watched from a distance until we left. I waved, a lump in my throat. Because it was their kind of stewardship ethic, as much as any breeding programs or other conservation efforts, that has kept the whooping crane from oblivion. Each year, spring and fall, those beautiful, vulnerable creatures cross the continent, exposed to the choices of many thousands of people. And, like the farmers who hurried out to check us, those people choose to leave them in peace and protect them from those who wouldn't.

Lately I've heard that some whooping cranes have started summering in central Alberta. Imagine: someday, they may nest among us again. Like sandhills, whooping cranes ride thermals too. Spiralling every higher, glistening white against the blue, they must look like angels ascending toward heaven. Reminders, perhaps, of our better angels.

MAKING MAGIC

A stillness comes over the natural world each August as birds cease their territorial singing and the year's crop of fledglings quietly fatten on the summer bounty of bugs and berries. Noise has its purpose in spring when territories need to be defended and mates attracted, but it only serves to draw the attention of predators once the youngsters are out and about.

I sat one day and looked up into the trees, contemplating that almost deathlike calm. Aspen leaves glowed in the sun, shaped into a paisley mosaic by the overlap of light and shadow. Pine needles reached out of the forest gloom for their share of sunlight. The forest floor was a dappled dance of late purple asters, fading grasses and berry-covered shrubs. The world was verdant and alive, but so still as to seem a lifeless diorama of itself.

Even in that calm, however, life shimmered everywhere. Each leaf – millions upon millions of them – was pulling gases out of the air into translucent cells where billions of tiny chloroplasts, like microscopic solar panels, trapped the light of the sun. Each chloroplast was using that transmuted sunshine to change carbon dioxide, extracted from the air, and water and trace minerals, drawn up from the forest soil, into living matter.

Medieval alchemists frequently poisoned themselves or went bankrupt in their quest to find a way to change other substances into gold – an inert metal. But no human alchemy could ever equal the magic that unfolds silently in the leaves that shade our summer afternoons – sunshine, air and water converted not just into energy, but into life itself.

While I watched the flickering mystery of the forest canopy overhead, down beneath the forest floor a secret society of roots was probing into the dark of the earth, pulling water out of the soil and feeding it into the wood cells that pipe it up the trees to the leaves. Insects foraged among the green canopy; in devouring living leaves they were turning plant matter into protein and chitin. And the quiet birds hunting those insects would transmute them, in turn, into living muscle and fat. When forest birds migrate, their tiny bodies are entirely composed of new life that arose from photosynthesis in the leaves among which they were hatched. They may fly above it, but they can never leave the forest because they are entirely made of it. Those are actually colourful bits of forest that migrate to faraway places each fall. Fancy that.

In the stillness of that summer afternoon only a dappled green glow offered my senses any hint of the photosynthetic miracle in which I was immersed. We aren't wired to sense the humming life of plant cells. Just beyond the edge of the forest I could hear the sounds of children at play, oblivious to the everyday magic in the leaves shading their play, even though it gave life to everything around them. It's strange, the things we just take for granted.

By midwinter it can be even harder to sense that magic. Trees are leafless. Snow covers the forest floor. Most of the birds are gone to warmer places. But the magic isn't gone; it's simply hidden.

Last summer's leaves moulder on the forest floor. Fungi and bacteria are turning what remains of their living tissue into yet more forms of life. Many of the tree's roots have died back too, leaving carbon residues to become part of the soil. Frozen tree trunks pipe no water out of the ground; no need to anyway, because the branches above are bare.

But even on the gloomiest days of the coldest winters, the mystery lives on. Live plant cells, nearly dormant, wait in leaf buds and tree bark and roots for the balance between day length and night length to shift. When the right amount of light reaches the waiting cells, and when warming soil releases water to the waiting roots, chemical messages shuttle through each tree and the buds awaken, and leaves unfurl, and chloroplasts begin their silent work, and life explodes again.

We can count on it. It's the green magic of nature that creates, and re-creates, the world we live in, the air we breathe and almost everything we find beautiful.

At a time when our hasty consumption of carbon fuels has filled the air with so much carbon dioxide that it's throwing the world's climates into chaos, we're told that we need to plant more trees. Good idea: photosynthesis enables trees to take carbon out of the air and turn it into wood.

But we shouldn't need such pragmatic reasons to create more woodlands. The world can never have enough magic – especially the life-renewing alchemy of photosynthesis. And it's easy to be part of that magic, after all. Anyone can plant a tree.

A MATTER OF TIMING

In October the smell of decomposing chlorophyll fills the forest as days grow shorter and frosts more frequent. The birdless woods go briefly yellow; then the wind takes the leaves away. Hunting season comes and the missing leaves reveal themselves on the forest floor, dry as cornflakes, frustrating hunters who hope to sneak up close to deer.

Bambi, according to author Felix Salten, was grateful for the timing of leaf fall: "O, how kind last year's leaves are! They do their duty so well and are so alert and watchful.... And they give warning in advance of every danger."

Our human tradition of hunting deer after harvest season aligns with each annual bounty of fallen leaves to make hunting more uncertain and escape more likely. It's a matter of fortuitous timing – just one of thousands of overlapping events that make the natural world work.

Not all those fallen leaves end up on the forest floor. In southern Alberta, where poplar forests form golden galleries along prairie rivers, the wind blows harder than farther north. Leaves dance along river floodplains until many of them light in the water. Good timing: autumn rivers flow slowly. Instead of washing away, the leaves accumulate in increasingly sodden drifts in back eddies and shallows until, eventually, they sink.

What a lucky coincidence. Autumn's short days barely warm those prairie rivers. Where summer's heat and sunshine yielded a bounteous harvest of algae and other aquatic plants to sustain the bacteria, fungi and invertebrates that fish need for food, sun-starved autumn rivers no longer produce much food. Fortuitously, that annual subsidy from fallen leaves arrives just in time. Through the long winter, the decomposing leaves feed micro-organisms, insects and fishes until the days grow long and warm again in spring.

Fortunate timing. It's no less fortunate for the poplars that Alberta's climate produces spring floods in late May and early June. When melting snows and spring rains send brown flood waters churning down our river valleys, the same poplars whose fallen leaves helped deer escape hunters and fed the river ecosystem all winter are green again. Seed buds burst on female poplars in early June, setting billions of cotton-like seeds adrift on the wind. Just like the falling leaves a few months earlier, many of those fluffy seeds light on the surface of the river.

Perfect timing; natural river flows subside through June. The ebbing flood waters reveal fresh new deposits of silt, sand and gravel on every point bar. The poplar seeds lodge on the wet, new material and take root. The new deposits lack competing vegetation to shade the baby poplars or compete with them for water. And the next generation of poplar forest is born – even as old trees pile up in logjams on the outside curves of eroding riverbanks. It's like a perfect conspiracy between river and forest.

If poplars released their seeds a month earlier or a month later, river-valley forests would have little hope of renewing themselves because they would miss that perfect moment when new, wet seed beds glisten in the spring sun beside an ebbing river. And there would be no leaves to warn the deer or feed the winter fishes. In fact, on rivers like the St. Mary's, where irrigation dams have changed the timing of floods, forests are gradually disappearing.

We tend to think of natural selection as being how individual species evolve, but in fact it contains countless feedback loops that link organisms and processes together. River ecosystems need poplars; poplars need river ecosystems. Through millennia, they have become synchronized with one another. Nature's timing has nothing to do with random luck.

Late each April the first poplar buds burst and new leaves poke out. Instantly, triggered by scent cues released by the new leaves, insects appear in the canopy. Perfect timing; earlier insects would starve. And virtually the same week, orange-crowned warblers appear, having timed their migration home from the tropics just in time to feed on the first canopy insects of the year. The rivers flow by; but all are linked.

Timing is everything. Robins and kingbirds nest in those poplars when insect populations peak. They fledge their young in late July, just in time for nearby saskatoons and raspberries to appear: perfect food to fatten their young for the fall migration. If berries should appear too soon or too late, fewer young birds survive the southward journey. But day length signals are the same each year; nature usually gets its timing right.

Usually.

Edmonton botanist Elisabeth Beaubien has monitored the phenology (seasonal timing) of common Alberta plants for several decades. She has found that as Alberta's climate warms, many species now flower and produce seeds or fruit days, or even weeks, earlier than they used to. Animals that rely on day-length cues for migration or breeding may have problems if bugs and berries no longer appear when they need them.

The complexity, productivity and beauty of Alberta's wild ecosystems is a matter of timing – syncopated rhythms, harmonies and chords arising from the meshing of countless living instruments over thousands of years. Predictable seasonal signals tie nature together in a living symphony with near-perfect timing.

Climate change, river modification or land uses can change those signals. The consequences could prove discordant.

CITY CRITTERS

People live in town and animals live in the country. At least that's how it used to be. But as Alberta's cities metastasize into sprawling infestations of asphalt, vinyl and strip malls that consume ever more of what remains of wildlife habitat, nature appears to be changing the rules. The wildlife is moving into town. Some of our new neighbours may take some getting used to.

I recently unearthed the scrapbooks of nature-related clippings that I kept as a preteen birdwatcher growing up in Calgary. In the mid-1960s, the big story each year was the increasing number of mallards staying in the city all winter. The Bearspaw Dam, completed a decade earlier, had created open water conditions by releasing water from the lower levels of its new reservoir. Downstream from Inglewood, the river was further warmed by releases of effluent from oil refineries and the city's sewage treatment plant. The river no longer vanished under ice each winter.

Open water made it possible for ducks to overwinter;

waste grain in nearby wheat fields and feedlots made it worthwhile. In the early 1960s, well-meaning hunting clubs and others, worried about the ducks starving in late winter, began feeding programs that led, by 1966, to well more than 15,000 mallards lingering on the Bow River each winter. The feeding programs ended but the ducks and, eventually, Canada geese stayed on. Today, flights of waterfowl shuttling between feedlots and stubble fields to open water patches are a regular part of winter life in Alberta's big cities.

The same 1960s-vintage scrapbooks informed me that Americans were panicking over the impending extinction of the bald eagle because of DDT poisoning. To a young birdwatcher, a bald eagle sighting was a major event. Today, thanks to abundant wintering waterfowl, the dark silhouettes of roosting eagles line most major urban rivers where dams and sewage discharges keep the water open all winter. Eagles are city birds now.

Ravens too. When a friend of mine turned up at a Calgary Bird Club meeting in 1968 with the report of a raven in Fish Creek Provincial Park, he encountered skeptical head shaking. Almost rendered extinct by poisons spread to fight rabies in foxes during the mid-1950s, ravens were rare during my youth, confined to the outer valleys of the Rocky Mountains. Not so today: dozens of ravens call Edmonton, Red Deer, Calgary and Lethbridge home.

The abundance of carrion-scavenging ravens may be partly due to another recent urban immigrant: deer. Scarce even in rural areas during the mid-20th century, populations of both mule and white-tailed deer boomed through the end of that century and the beginning of this one. With increased deer numbers out in the country, predators such as cougar and coyote are thriving as well. By the 1980s, deer were regular sights in the newer subdivisions around the edges of large cities, attracted probably as much by safety from the more hesitant predators as by the edible landscaping. Today, deer live year-round in our larger urban parks and the surrounding neighbourhoods.

And the predators have overcome their earlier hesitation: dozens of coyotes now live in Alberta's larger cities. They feed on winter-weakened deer, poorly stored garbage, stray cats and another recent immigrant to the big city: jackrabbits.

Most of the native animals that have adopted our cities as their homes are drawn there by food and safety from predators. Deer and elk, in particular, are quick to adjust to changes in hunting pressure. Even though the odd cougar shows up in city parks, most of the larger predators still prefer a bit less human company than they have to endure in urban settings. And the increasing number of humans building homes on acreages around the edges of cities means that human hunters are increasingly unwelcome there too.

No surprise that ungulates, jackrabbits and other prey animals are choosing to snuggle up to us. We can expect more cougars in our cities over the coming years. In fact, it shouldn't be a surprise when the first grizzly turns up in Calgary's Fish Creek Provincial Park or Lethbridge's river valley, or when Sherwood Park residents waken one day to the sound of wolves howling. Urban life isn't just for people anymore.

Neil Young sang about "Mother Nature on the run in the 1970s." As sprawl continues to chew away at the most productive wildlife habitats in prairie and foothills Alberta, Mother Nature is still on the run; many more species and habitats are at risk here than ever before. A study by Global Forest Watch released in January showed that Alberta has Canada's highest rate of habitat damage due to industrial and agricultural landscape fragmentation – more than two-thirds of the province is no longer healthy or productive for native wildlife.

Little wonder, then, that some of them are moving in with us.

MISSING BIRDS

The deep of winter would be a time of despair were it not for the sure promise of spring. The sky is empty of birds and each dawn is silent and cold. The sun barely rises before it begins again to set. But hope lives on, because we remember previous springs and anticipate the glory of the next one.

As a certified old-timer, I can now look back in memory at 66 springtimes when the world refilled itself with warmth and birdsong. No matter how dark and long the winter nights, there should be no doubt left in my soul. But doubt there is – fear, in fact.

I worry about the missing birds.

Recently, I found some scribblers filled with my field notes from the early 1960s. I was an aspiring young naturalist then, thrilled by the diversity of birds that I found during sojourns into the wild edges of a much smaller Calgary. One early June day I stood on the old wooden bridge beside the Shaganappi Golf Course and peered down into the shrubbery below. I can actually still remember the smell – wolf willows and chokecherries in bloom and the green scents of new leaves – and the amazement I felt at finding birds I'd never imagined lived in my hometown. From that one perch I recorded three veeries, a brown thrasher, two catbirds, six yellow warblers, three least fly-catchers, four house wrens and several robins – all singing on newly claimed nesting territories. It was a chaos of birdsong.

Later that month, my notes record a bicycle ride into the farmland near Chestermere Lake. Long-billed cur-lews and marbled godwits harassed me as I explored relict tracts of native prairie. Horned larks, vesper and savannah sparrows and meadowlarks provided the day's soundtrack, and I listened, transfixed, as I heard for the first time the thin, descending tinkle of a Sprague's pipit's flight song high in the prairie sky. That day's highlight: two nesting pairs of burrowing owls – right inside the city limits!

Good memories for a cold winter day, and reassurance that when spring once more washes north across the con-tinent it will bring new greenery and migrating birds too. At least it should. The dwindling of hope arises from the shocking reality that many of those birds won't be coming home this spring.

Rachel Carson published *Silent Spring*, warning the world about the impact of organochlorine pesticides on bird life, the same year I recorded all that avian abundance. The world listened; DDT and related chemicals have been banned for years. But we are facing a second, and worse, silent spring today.

A study in the journal *Science* recently analyzed monitoring data on 529 North American bird species. Some – such as peregrine falcons, white pelicans and others whose populations plummeted in the 1960s because of the effects of DDT – have increased since those poisons were banned. But birds we never dreamed of worrying about are now in trouble. Native sparrows, finches, blackbirds and warblers are simply disappearing. Even barn swallows – which used to nest in every farm outbuilding and under every bridge in the province – are now listed with curlews, pipits and many other species as at risk of disappearing. Burrowing owls are virtually gone from Alberta.

It's hard to miss the birds you never knew, and that's perhaps what worries this old-timer most. Nobody under the age of 40 today ever experienced the glorious spring choruses I used to simply take for granted. Abnormal feels normal if it's all you've ever had.

But hope is always an option, if we're willing to act.

After all, the ban on organochlorines brought back the nearly extinct peregrine. Remember acid rain? Forcing industry to scrub its exhaust gases dialled that problem right down. Once-dead lakes and forests have now recovered. Remember the ozone hole? When we banned chlorofluorocarbons it began to heal. Bad things needn't last.

Bird numbers are collapsing for many reasons – outdoor cats, brightly lit high-rises and towers that kill night-flying migrants, habitat loss. But the big culprit, just as it was in the 1960s, is poisoning. Neonicotinoids are a new class of hyper-effective insect poisons aggressively marketed to farmers by the multinationals that profit from them. They kill entire food chains. That's why some EU countries have banned them and Canada is moving – very slowly – toward tighter regulation.

Using poisons to produce food is a truly cockeyed concept, especially when those toxins kill everything else that makes life worth living. Chemicals so profoundly lethal as neonicotinoids should simply be banned. Totally. Immediately.

Dark thoughts in mid-winter – but not entirely hopeless. The song-filled glory chronicled in my old field notes could be tomorrow's springtimes too. We just need to stop poisoning the birds.

IN DEFENCE OF SNOW

Winter is part of the deal if you're an Albertan, and winter means snow. Snow is a good thing if you own skis but not so good if you have a long driveway. Regardless of one's preferences, snow is important – both for wildlife and for us.

At least our snow isn't the wet, sodden stuff that attacks eastern Canada, crushing roofs and sending snow shovellers to emergency rooms with heart attacks. The dry air and hard cold of our continental climate usually yields lighter flakes. This powder lasts only until the wind rearranges it into hard-packed drifts or a thaw changes the fluff to snowball snow before recrystallizing it and leaving a frozen crust on top. By late winter, Alberta snow shovellers are usually sick of the stuff.

Out in the woods and fields, winter snowpack can be hard on wildlife too. Usually it's hard winters, not predators, that cause big die-offs of deer and elk. Dry twigs and cured grass just don't cut it as fuel for animals that have to burn off their fat reserves both to keep warm and to plow through the deepening drifts. Cold winters with deep snow can knock deer and elk herds back for years, especially if a late spring blizzard administers a *coup de grâce* to the starving animals.

But that's actually good news for scavengers. Deer that die in the snow feed a wide variety of animals, from coyotes, eagles and ravens down to weasels, deer mice and chickadees. A hard winter is a godsend for creatures who depend for food on the remains of other animals.

Even some ungulates benefit from deep snow. Long-legged moose, for example, have no trouble navigating drifts that bog down the shorter-legged deer and elk. The oversized hooves of caribou work like snowshoes to keep them from sinking into snowdrifts. Moose and caribou both seek out snow too deep for wolves and cougars. Rather than waste energy bellying through the drifts, the predators hunt elk and deer where the snow is shallower.

Skiers and snowshoers, like caribou, thrive in deep snow. The rest of us are like elk; we can't wait for it to be gone. So it might seem fortuitous that, here in Alberta, we often get winters with little snow. When blizzards miss us and chinook winds sweep away the drifts, jaded snow shovellers and elk alike have reason to rejoice.

But that lack of snow means a killing winter for many other creatures. Mice, voles and squirrels, for example, rely on snow as insulation to keep ground level temperatures moderate and to hide them from hungry hawks and owls. Less snow means not only greater predation risk but more heat loss too – which means they need more food just when it's scarcest. Winters without snow are even tougher for snowshoe hares, jackrabbits and ptarmigan, whose winter survival strategy is to turn white. Without snow, those creatures stand out like white flags of surrender and are quickly picked off by predators.

Writers strive to avoid redundancy; at this point I'm tired of the word "snow." Unfortunately, our language gives us few alternative nouns. I should have written this in Inuktitut. Igor Krupnik, an anthropologist at Washington's Smithsonian Institution, has documented at least 53 different words for snow among the Inuit of Nunavik, reinforcing an observation made a century earlier by Franz Boas. People whose culture evolved in winter regions have long known what snow ecologists are only now discovering: over the course of a winter, snow becomes more than one thing. From the soft, newly settled snow after a blizzard to the wind-hardened drifts that Blackfoot hunters once used to trap bison to the recrystallized "sugar snow" under spring crusts, there are many kinds of snow. Each contributes in its own way to shaping not just the ecology but even the hydrology of northern landscapes such as ours.

Most of the water in prairie rivers, after all, originates as winter snow. A deep snowpack doesn't just store a lot of water, it insulates the ground below and keeps it from freezing deep or hard. In the spring much of the water that drains from thawing drifts soaks into the quickly thawed soil rather than running off over frozen ground. As groundwater, that melted snow becomes a gift that keeps on giving to the rivers for months to come. Without deep winter snow, however, soil freezes hard and the frost goes deep. It's a double whammy: there is less meltwater and more of it escapes as surface runoff.

Some pundits have suggested that global warming might produce better conditions for prairie agriculture. It's not that simple. Hydrologists such as the University of Saskatchewan's John Pomeroy warn that climate change is yielding shallower snowpacks in the prairies. Winter precipitation increasingly comes as rain rather than snow. That's good news for deer, elk and we snow shovellers. But it's bad news for a lot of other wildlife – and for our water supply too.

ICE AND FIRE

Winter: trees stand leafless in the snow and animals seek shelter from bitter winds. Most birds have left; most of those that stay survive by scavenging the remains of the season's victims. Nights are long; days are barren.

Winter can be as hard on us as on other living things. But we are a determined and optimistic species. At the darkest time of the year we decorate our homes with light and colour. We invite family and friends to elaborate feasts. This may be a season of scarcity, but we are defiant: we splurge on gifts as if abundance will never end.

Complicit in our stubborn refusal to surrender to the season are the evergreens: spruce, fir, pine and other trees that keep their green foliage through the winter. Most Canadian homes greet the winter solstice with a sweet-scented tree in the living room, a promise of nature's future abundance.

During September 2017, however, most of the evergreens in Waterton Lakes National Park burned up. For a few days the Kenow fire dominated Alberta news, just as the 2016 Fort McMurray wildfire and the 2011 Slave Lake fire took over our collective consciousness as other forests exploded into flame and smoke. Waterton's Christmas was less a white one that year than a grey one as the park's famous winds whipped charred tree bark and ash across the snow. Winter is hard; Waterton's winters became a bit harder after the flames swept through.

Ice and fire: winter may be a time of dying, when hypothermia, starvation and freezing are constant threats, but we know how to get through it. Fire is another matter. Prairie, parkland, northern forests and mountain fastnesses: for millennia fire has shaped and renewed all our Alberta places. But each fire still comes as a shock. We don't seem capable of seeing nature's flames as bringing renewal, only disaster.

As Waterton's fire came to the end of its run, the area's Member of Parliament did a helicopter tour of the park. In a Facebook video, Foothills MP John Barlow said, predictably: "The damage to Waterton is devastating," and went on to report that 70 per cent of the park's forests were lost. That's how we always talk about wildfire.

The emphasis on damage is warranted where fences, buildings and houses are concerned. Five homes burned down outside the park. But real-time rhetoric around fire usually fails to acknowledge that those flames are both natural and necessary. Fire, like winter, wind, floods and rain, is an ecological process that helps renew and diversify our natural places. It's really only a problem when we put flammable structures in its way.

I visited Waterton on September 23 while the fire was still smouldering. I found bright green spikes of fescue and oatgrass sprouting from blackened prairie. Bluebirds, killdeers and meadowlarks foraged among the ashes, fattening on scorched insects before their migration south. Biologists monitoring the burn told me that no Waterton bear went to bed hungry that winter; they had gorged on carrion from animals that didn't escape the flames.

The following spring, park visitors marvelled at the bright green grass sprouting across blackened hills. Millions of aspen and poplar sprouts rose through the ashes from unburned root systems. Ground squirrels emerged from their fireproof burrows to blink in the spring sunshine; eagles and hawks were waiting. Pine cones, opened by the fire's heat, shed seeds into potassium-rich ash and scorched organic material, starting a next generation. Unburned patches, of which there were many, welcomed returning migratory birds. The elk, sheep and deer that sheltered there grazed the new green growth on the nearby hillsides.

Insects, attracted by the scent of dead wood, invaded the standing spars and lay eggs. Woodpeckers soon followed, including the rare black-backed woodpecker that relies on fire to create its preferred habitat. In the coming years, woodpecker holes will house bats, flying squirrels and bluebirds. Freed temporarily from competition for sun and water, the forest floors have erupted in greenery and flower. Mice, voles, owls and foxes thrive on the abundance.

It has become a different place, but very much a living place. Waterton was not destroyed; it was renewed, just as it had been repeatedly before. In 1998 another lightning-caused fire swept through the eastern part of the park; that earlier burn is now a green jungle of life. The forests that burned in 1998 and 2017 had sprouted after earlier fires. So it goes.

If there were no fires, we would have no Christmas trees. They evolved together. While we huddle against the cold this solstice season, we should celebrate Waterton's renewal by fire. For all the stress, fear and property losses it caused, it was nature's gift to us. One of many.

2

LAND MATTERS

GODS' FOOTPRINTS

If you could hold a black-throated green warbler in your hand, it would be soft to the touch and strangely light. Barely as long as an avocado, the slender greenish bird with a black neck and brilliant yellow face staring up at you would weigh less than two nickels. Just feathers, hollow bones, some muscle and a fierce little heart.

Its dark eyes would watch you with a bright, intense gaze. The little bird's heart would be racing because it would likely feel that it had been caught by a predator. It might be more apt, if warblers could formulate that concept (and who knows – perhaps they can), for it to believe that it was looking into the face of a god.

Gods, after all, have the power to create and destroy. And we humans are capable of both. A recently released report by the Alberta Biodiversity Monitoring Institute (ABMI) profiles the black-throated green warbler as a species whose numbers have dropped by 20 per cent because of our powers of destruction.

Fortunately for Alberta's warblers, the chances are almost nil that you will ever get to hold one in your hand and feel, in its nearly weightless fragility, the awful power and responsibility of a god. But perhaps that's actually too bad, considering the harm of which we lesser gods are capable.

Not only might you never hold one, you may never see one either. Black-throated green warblers sing, forage and raise their young in old boreal forests – the kind that loggers describe as "over-mature" – and eat spruce budworms and other insects in the most ancient conifers. They flit and scurry far overhead, obscured by the interlocking branches of the canopy. You might never even hear one. In the green, living stillness of the northern forest, the black-throated green is among the birds with the softest of voices: a short series of high-pitched notes.

So we live in our Alberta and they live in theirs. In summer that is; in winter they can be found foraging for food in the forests of Central America and Mexico. Late in March, having fattened for the spring migration, the birds become restless with an avian version of homesickness. Those little hearts propel those tiny bodies across Mexico, the whole length of the continental US and into southern Canada. They arrive in Alberta in late May just in time for the first big eruption of boreal insect life. High in the tree-tops, flashes of living colour amid the dark canopy, the warblers build nests, lay eggs and raise young.

But sometimes, when they finally arrive home, it isn't there anymore. Boreal forests are constantly renewed by wildfires, so to some extent the birds are used to finding last year's forest gone. They simply search for another stand of trees more than a century old. That search, however, becomes increasingly difficult as logging companies continue cutting down forests that will never be allowed to grow ancient again.

The ABMI's study, entitled "Status of Human Footprint in Alberta," used a number of data sources to measure how much of our province has become unusable to nature because it has been developed for our use – the "human footprint." The human footprint in Alberta's boreal forest region increased from 15 per cent to more than 18 per cent in the first decade and a half of the 21st century, with most of that owing to forestry.

Almost one-fifth of the habitat once available to black-throated green warblers is now gone. The replanted trees will be cut again before they grow old enough for the birds to use.

It's even worse for other wildlife elsewhere in Alberta.

Almost 30 per cent of the province is now lost under our human footprint: little more than two-thirds of the province is available to nature. In some regions it's even worse: 78 per cent of the parkland region has been appropriated for human use and almost 60 per cent of the grassland region, mostly because we've plowed the land under for agriculture. While boreal Alberta still has its black-throated green warblers, most prairie birds are now classified as threatened or endangered. Some, like the burrowing owl, are almost extinct.

With such big footprints, isn't it time we start treading more gently?

The ABMI study is only the most recent report showing the impact of rampant development and thoughtless self-absorption. We might argue that this is our Alberta and we can do as we like. Those tiny birds, however, could rightly respond that this is also their Alberta and they never chose us as their gods. We did that. But those who assume godlike powers have responsibilities too, not the least of which is to care about Creation – and to care for it. We might never hold a black-throated green warbler in our hands, but we hold its fate there.

WORKING LANDSCAPES

Talk to anybody employed in forestry and you'll likely hear the term "working forest." That's where feller-bunchers and chainsaws convert living forests into trucks loaded with logs – most of northern and western Alberta, in other words.

Global Rangelands, an outreach initiative sponsored by colleges and universities in the western US, extends the concept to everywhere else: "When we talk about working landscapes we are talking about the areas between cities or towns and natural areas with limited continuous use by people. Rural areas, which often are dominated by intensive or extensive agricultural, forestry or other natural resources–based economies, are generally a part of a working landscape."

The working landscape is a concept that appeals to our materialistic culture. Why let things go to waste if they can be put to work generating profit? "Deep ecologists" – who see humans as just one of many equal components of nature – may scoff at the idea, but more pragmatic environmentalists seem comfortable enough with it. The late Francis Gardner, a respected foothills conservationist and rancher, once described his family's ranch to me as a "working wilderness." He and his wife Bonnie saw their role as stewards of an intact ecosystem, and the wolves and grizzly bears living there as indicators – albeit challenging ones – of their success.

Advocates of the working landscapes concept argue that we can make productive economic use of the land while still retaining its biodiversity and ecological functions. That's an attractive ideal, and one worth working toward. The results, unfortunately, sometimes fail to match the rhetoric.

Just as a working person is better than an idle one, and working parents often get more respect than those who stay home to raise their kids, the idea of a working landscape attaches economic and cultural worth to a landscape that many would otherwise see just as idle scenery. But it's predicated on a value system based on domination and subjugation. The darker side to the "working" metaphor, when applied to living places, is that it assumes a moral right of corporate interests to colonize and repurpose whole ecosystems. If it's a working landscape, then by implication the logging companies, oil and gas industry and livestock producers who put it to work should get to decide what happens there. Others – especially Indigenous Peoples, environmentalists and recreationists who might like it the way it is – should butt out, or at least be grateful when the dominant class grants them the chance to offer humble suggestions.

Another dark side of the working landscape concept is that it's founded on the conceit that leaving land alone is somehow wasteful. Corporate interests and their political protectors, for example, often describe establishing parks as "sterilizing" the land – a deliberately hostile verb. In truth, land is only truly sterilized when buried under roads and asphalt, or cropped so hard its soils can only be kept fertile with chemicals. Sadly, our working landscapes include a lot of that kind of land.

None of those working landscapes ever applied for the job. But in a society that accrues material wealth by exploiting natural resources, land is simply forced to do work we've assigned it. The same business interests who are so enamoured of "working landscape" also love the term "multiple use" and often mention both in the same breath. We expect land to do several jobs at once: produce wood for mills, surrender oil and gas to be burned, feed cows and be mined for its gravel, coal and other subterranean assets. So these aren't just working landscapes – they're multi-tasking ones, toiling away at tasks they never signed up for.

When a human being is given no choice but to work at a job he or she never asked for, that's called slavery.

By that definition, there are no working landscapes, only enslaved ones. The only free landscapes would be our parks and protected areas and the remaining bits of the rest of the province that haven't yet been indentured to one or more resource companies. Far from having been sterilized, protected areas are places where land is allowed to do its real work.

Because every one of those landscapes was already hard at work. They work at capturing rain and snow and filtering it through green vegetation and spongy soils into groundwater aquifers that feed springs, rivers and downstream communities. They grow diverse plant communities that pull carbon dioxide from the air and put oxygen back in. They work tirelessly at providing habitat for native plants, animals and fish, and spiritual renewal for many thousands of people. They hold memory, meaning and life.

Alberta's enslaved landscapes were never unemployed to start with. And most of the jobs we force them to do impair their ability to do their real work. That's how slavery works; it makes bosses rich by stealing the energies of their slaves.

KEEPING IT TOGETHER

When our son headed off to the South American rain-forest, one of the items on his checklist was a water purifying system. He didn't want to pick up the wrong hitchhikers. The helpful sales agent at his outdoors store warned him not to rely on iodine tablets except in emergencies. "You don't want to kill your gut flora," he said. "Then you'd really have a problem."

Few of us spend much time thinking about what lives inside of us. Maybe it's our reductionist Western science tradition that makes us isolate human beings from the rest of nature. But in doing so we're just fooling ourselves. We are not alone. Far from it.

Each of us hosts an estimated 100 trillion micro-organisms on and in our bodies. We are not individuals; we are ecosystems. Our gut contains ten times as many microbial cells as body cells. Those little organisms help us digest efficiently, influence our moods, keep us from getting too fat and protect our bodies against colonization by harmful bacteria. We, in turn, provide all those microbes with a temperature-controlled, food-rich and warm environment in which to thrive.

Little creatures that live in our eyelids graze the vast plains of our skin each night, cleaning up harmful bacteria and getting rid of dead body cells. Other creatures only visit, like the mosquitoes who sip our blood and the viruses and bacteria that propagate in our bodies and then migrate to others through handshakes and sneezes.

We're all in this together. If the recent medical concept of fecal matter transplants seems horrifying, it's only because we tend to think of germs as enemies, rather than community members. Once we understand our bodies as complex communities of life, it starts to make sense to ask if any community members are missing and whether it might be helpful to get them back – where they belong.

In school we're taught about symbiotic relationships between organisms as something unusual. Lichens, for example, are plants composed of both an alga and a fungus. Isn't that weird? Bark beetles carry fungus spores that attack the wood of the trees where beetles lay their eggs; when the eggs hatch, the baby beetles survive because the fungi infection makes the wood edible. Neat.

But there is nothing unusual or exotic about that at all.

It is the way the world works. And when we fail to acknowledge the complex webs of interconnections that make things what they are, we tend to make mistakes we don't recognize and get results we never intended.

My wife and I moved our family to Okotoks for a couple of years in the 1990s. Suburban and acreage development was rampant. To my ecologist's sensibilities, it was heart-rending to see the rate at which bulldozers and scrapers were peeling the top off the fescue prairie and replacing it with roads, lawns and monster homes. "It's okay," I recall being reassured. "Once the development is in, they'll plant the grass again."

I knew better. Prairie is not grass, any more than we are made solely of human cells. I decided to salvage some prairie and try to educate at least some of the neighbours so they would know better too. Weekends would see me wrestling matted lumps of spiky grass into the back of our van and hurrying home to wedge them against other salvaged clods in what the kids were soon calling our "front yard prairie." Passing neighbours looked askance or rolled their eyes as the patch of rough grassland grew in front of our house. I put up a little sign explaining what it was and listing all the plants that actually lived in what looked, at first glance, like a bunch of unmowed grass.

In the first season I found more than 70 such plants: from little drought-tolerant mosses hidden beneath the clumps of rough fescue to buffalo bean, prairie crocus, wood lily, needlegrass, oatgrass, shrubby cinquefoil and pasture sage. Every time I thought I had a complete list, another frond or flower would appear and another name went on the list.

Those native Alberta plants were dying all around Okotoks, to be replaced with seed mixes containing three or four commercial grass varieties. They still are. The people moving to the countryside to raise their kids close to nature didn't realize they were killing whole communities to do so, replacing them with facsimiles. They saw prairie as one thing – grass – rather than the real thing: a complex community of native plants, insects, microbes and fungi.

Health providers avoid prescribing too many antibiotics for the same reason the store clerk warned our son about iodine tablets. Kill the community that lives in your gut, and you lose that community's ability to keep us healthy and alive. The same thing happens when we sterilize Alberta's native grasslands by blithely ripping them up in the misguided belief that we can always plant grass again.

We are not alone. We'd better hope we don't end up that way.

BUILDING WHERE WE SHOULDN'T

If you want to see elk or wolves in Banff or Jasper national parks this winter, here's a tip: look for an alluvial fan. Alluvial fans develop wherever a creek running down a steep drainage flows out into a larger valley. Over the centuries those creeks deposit countless tons of eroded rock, building fan-shaped landforms at the edges of larger river valleys. The big valleys that our highways follow through the Rockies trap the flow of dozens of such drainages.

Mountains are constantly falling apart as their rock weathers and erodes. Gravity pulls all the loose bits downhill, where they accumulate on avalanche paths, talus slopes and valley floors. Tons and tons of loose material gradually fill those steep mountain valleys.

Winter snows and spring rains flush the smallest bits away when creeks flood each spring. Gravity gives flood waters a lot of power. The faster the stream's flow, the more rock and gravel it can move. Arriving at the valley floor, those flood waters lose momentum and have to deposit most of their load. Those accumulated deposits are what form alluvial fans.

Once every few years, much bigger floods pour out those steep valleys. That's when most of the stockpiled rock debris gets flushed down to the alluvial fans at the bottom of each drainage. During those big flood years, streams often change course completely as their former channels fill with new deposits. An alluvial fan is a mosaic of abandoned creek channels of varying ages, gradually filling in the mouth of the valley.

That dynamic, shifting nature is why alluvial fans support rich patchworks of vegetation – from old spruce stands, through young poplar and willow thickets, to grassy gravel flats near the active stream channel. That diversity of vegetation is one reason why wildlife like alluvial fans.

Years ago I worked on the original wildlife inventories of Banff and Jasper national parks. We counted wildlife from frogs to bats, songbirds and bighorns to determine which habitats were most important.

When we tallied up our results at the end of six years, we found that alluvial fans and stream floodplains were by far the most productive wildlife habitats. Not only are they critical range for wintering elk and deer and the predators that feed on them, they are essential year-round for rodents, songbirds, bears and other wildlife – far more important than adjacent forests and mountainsides.

But their gentle slopes and well-drained soils make these sites irresistible for developers too. The town of Banff sits on parts of two alluvial fans. Almost every other alluvial fan in Banff's Bow valley has a road, campground, motel or other development on it. Jasper has fared better – only a few of the fans along the broader Athabasca valley have been developed.

Good land-use planning would have left those alluvial fans for wildlife and put our infrastructure on stable landforms such as the glacial terraces that line many mountain valleys. But developers and planners had the benefit of neither wildlife inventories nor bitter experience in the early 20th century when key decisions were being made.

The 2013 flood certainly provided the bitter experience. Those steep mountain valleys had been accumulating stockpiles of broken mountain for decades, awaiting the big flood that would flush them down to the alluvial fans. When that big flood arrived, our stuff was in the way.

Canmore – my hometown – had spent three decades covering the alluvial fan of Cougar Creek with housing. That wiped out some of the valley's best wildlife habitat; one neighbourhood is even called "Elk Run."

Town planners thought they could protect those houses by confining the creek to a single drainage channel. But steep mountain creeks aren't just water when it floods – they are water, mud, gravel, boulders and trees. Cougar Creek filled the engineered channel with rock debris from its steep upper valley and washed away the banks so it could cut a new channel. Because that's how alluvial fans work.

The repair costs in the Bow valley alone will exceed $100 million. Mostly, those repairs have involved putting the creeks back where we want them. But these are alluvial fans; the creeks won't stay there. Engineers and civil planners are starting to understand that when steep creeks flood it isn't just water they have to deal with; it's almost unimaginable amounts of rock and mud. But their solutions still seem to involve turning a dynamic piece of landscape into a static one.

That won't work. The mountains are still falling apart, and those steep valleys continue to stockpile all the debris high in the headwaters, waiting for the next big flood to flush it out. That flood will come. Mother Nature always wins. The only lasting solution is to move our stuff out of places that are meant for wildlife.

CREEK REPAIRS

This past September I signed up for a volunteer work bee with Trout Unlimited Canada (TUC) and spent a day with about a dozen people I had never met before, including an oil engineer, a banker, a couple of retired guys and some young biologists. They were good folks – the kind who give back rather than simply keep taking.

Our work site was seven kilometres up Hidden Creek from its confluence with the Oldman River. We started with a bracing ford of a very cold river, emerging onto an abandoned logging road on the opposite bank. Back in dry footwear, we followed the road up into a huge clear-cut.

The Oldman watershed was once one of the most beautiful places in Alberta, and it's still spectacular. It's all public land. But it was immediately obvious, as we tramped our way through the stump-filled barrens left behind by a logging company, that we haven't treated it well. The clear-cuts at the mouth of Hidden Creek are immense.

And it isn't just loggers who use the Oldman hard.

Unlike on some other public land grazing allotments, the results of cattle mismanagement were all too evident. Good range managers leave at least 40 per cent of the grass standing at the end of each grazing season to keep vegetation healthy, protect the soil and provide winter forage for wildlife. But the upper Oldman's meadows looked like putting greens. They had been grazed almost to the roots.

The road curved up into a forested valley and started to hug the edge of the creek just downhill from more recent clear-cuts. Deeply gullied creeks drained out of those 2012 cutblocks where heavy rains had spilled off of the barren ground instead of soaking into forest soils like they formerly would have done. A fisheries biologist friend tells me that farther upstream, where loggers haven't yet stripped the trees away, similar creeks still have intact channels.

Recent rains had soaked the road and left it full of silty ponds that were gradually releasing mud into the otherwise pristine Hidden Creek. Why, I asked one of the TUC biologists, was this road still here? The loggers were finished, after all. Couldn't they have reclaimed it? He explained that although the area's land-use plan calls for an end to motorized use in the valley, the owners of those cattle wanted the road left in place so it would be easier to tend their cows and fences. That seemed a bit strange to me – the ranchers pay a pittance for their grazing permits. They have no property rights that would trump approved conservation plans for our public land.

Halfway in, the biologists pointed out where the stream gravel had been scoured out of a hollow about the size of a suitcase and piled up in a mound just downstream. It was a bull trout redd, or spawning nest. Until recently about 80 per cent of the Oldman drainage's surviving bull trout spawned in Hidden Creek. A threatened species, the bull trout is also Alberta's official provincial fish.

Bull trout only spawn where cold groundwater wells up into clean stream gravel. That groundwater keeps trout eggs from freezing in the winter and supplies eggs and fry with oxygen. Most of the Oldman headwaters have been logged so extensively and grazed so hard that their former spawning beds are now choked with silt and their ground-water flows disrupted. Hidden Creek was the last truly healthy trout stream surviving.

But flood waters draining from recent clear-cuts in the surrounding landscape have collapsed Hidden Creek's banks in several places. Mud now continually erodes into the spawning gravels. The number of bull trout redds has dropped by 70 per cent since the 2013 spring flood. Only five females spawned in 2018. None did in 2020.

Our work site, when we arrived, was part of the problem. Off-highway vehicle use had kept the logging road bare and muddy. That road should have been reclaimed when the logging was finished, but the grazing permit holder wanted it kept open. When the 2013 flood found a compacted road with no live vegetation to hold the soil together, it scoured part of it away. My (and your) tax money was then used to reroute the road so that cattle owners could continue using motorized vehicles – in an area closed to motorized vehicles. The resulting mess was left for us volunteers to fix.

It was encouraging to see that other volunteers had already repaired half the site the previous year, and their work had held up. We got the rest of it done. We spent our day pounding live willow stakes into the mud and using willow and poplar stems to create small retaining walls on the rest of the site. It was hard work, but it felt good to help restore a wounded creek.

Still, it seemed strange that our group included not one logger, off-roader or grazing permit holder.

STRIP MINES IN THE HEADWATERS

It looks like spectacular wild country, but some see it more as a big money sandwich.

The top layer of that sandwich is made up of alpine grasses, forget-me-not and stonecrop, glacier lilies and ancient, brave pines whose branches have been gnarled and weathered by centuries of wind. In summer, solitaires and blue grouse huddle against the ground to hatch their eggs while grizzlies dig out marmots from under lichen-encrusted boulders. Winter's howling winds scour snow into the trees below while bighorn sheep and elk eke out a survival ration of dry grass.

At the bottom layer, water that originated as snow-melt and rain, having seeped and dripped through shadowed layers of rock, emerges cold and clean in springs that feed small creeks whose floodplains are mosaics of spruce and meadow, birdsong and water chatter. Native westslope cutthroat trout rise for mayflies, and in the deeper shadows immense bull trout fin quietly above the clean gravels to which they return each summer to deposit their eggs.

And the middle of the sandwich? Unprocessed wealth: black, bituminous coal.

Perhaps it's not so much a sandwich as a sort of geological lasagna, with layers of coal intermixed with layers of shale and sandstone, and everything tending to run together once you slice into it. Whatever foodie metaphor one might choose, it's a big chunk of Alberta. High-grade coal deposits – ideal for feeding the coking ovens that produce the world's steel and other metals – crop out intermittently from south of the Crowsnest Pass to north of Grande Cache, a swath of land more than 850 km long and 5–20 km wide.

Hunters, anglers, hikers and naturalists think of it not as coal country, but as God's country. The bighorns, trout and other living things think of it as home. Multinational mining companies have been thinking about it a lot lately. That's why its future is an open question.

Up to 600,000 hectares of our headwaters – an area almost the size of Edmonton – are under lease today for possible future mountaintop strip mining. Setting aside the ethics of profiting from climate change, whether all those leases become actual mines will depend on whether mining companies like Teck Resources, Riversdale and Montem can rip the middle out of the sandwich without also destroying that green and lovely bighorn country on top and those sweet clear streams below. They probably can't.

Alberta's coal originated between 140 and 65 million years ago in lush, well-vegetated swamps that probably looked a lot like Jurassic Park. The North American continent floats on an immense plate and the Pacific Ocean lies on top of another one. The slow-motion collision between those plates pushed up the Rocky Mountains and gradually depressed the continent's interior. Layer after layer of dead vegetation became buried under new greenery. Sand and silt eroding from the young Rockies washed east onto the sinking swamps, burying the layers of peat. As the weight of new sediments grew heavier, the peat was compressed into coal beds layered with shale and sandstone.

The oldest coal deposits became part of the Front Ranges and foothills of the Rocky Mountains as those got pushed toward the sky 80–55 million years ago. The coal beds under today's plains are younger and of a lower grade – good enough for electricity production but too impure for firing blast furnaces used in steelmaking.

Alberta's first commercial mine opened near Lethbridge in 1874. Coal heated frontier homes, powered train locomotives and fuelled steam-powered farming and industrial equipment. Oil displaced coal for most of those purposes after the Second World War. Starting in 1962, however, coal became important again as utility companies like Calgary Power began stripping thermal coal from accessible deposits on the plains to generate electricity. By the turn of the century, about half of Alberta's electricity was coming from coal-fired electric plants.

But coal is a dirty fuel. It releases countless tons of carbon dioxide into our warming atmosphere and exposes downwind residents to particulate pollution. That's why Alberta's 2015 Climate Leadership Plan calls for coal-generated electricity to be phased out by 2030. In the first three years of the plan, Alberta's coal production decreased by more than one-third. As less-polluting energy sources take over, it might seem like the end of coal mining for Alberta.

But if that's the case, why have coal companies been taking out big coal leases along the edge of the Rockies?

✿

Metallurgical (coking) coal is used to fire blast furnaces in steel production. Thermal coal may be out of favour as a source of electricity, but the world's demand for steel isn't going away. The bituminous coal in Alberta's Front Ranges is ideal for coking. It's a lucrative export to overseas steel factories – where it pours carbon dioxide into the planet's atmosphere just the same as if we'd burned it here.

In most places where metallurgical coal is mined, giant machines scrape off vegetation and overburden to get at the coal-bearing strata. The coal is stripped out and the remaining rock debris pushed into spoil heaps. The resulting pits and rubble piles can be massive. As the companies exhaust parts of the mine, they are required to reclaim the site. That usually involves bulldozing the spoil heaps to slopes less than 27 per cent and then spraying fertilizer and seed on top to get vegetation established. Even then, toxic chemicals can leach into nearby streams for decades.

The Crowsnest Pass communities and Canmore and Nordegg all began as coal towns and still live with the legacy of abandoned mines. Grande Cache's boom–bust coal mines closed most recently in 2015. Bituminous coal is still mined at Coal Valley and the Cheviot mine, which opened south of Hinton when the nearby Luscar and Gregg River mines closed down. Alberta's metallurgical coal production is barely half the level it was five years ago, but Alberta Energy expects production to increase again in 2019 now that the Grande Cache mine has reopened, and with the start of production at the Vista mine just east of Hinton.

In spite of the recent downward trend, the June 2018 *Canadian Mining Journal* was almost breathless in its excitement over the prospects for new coking coal development in Alberta: "Canada is the world's third-largest exporter of metallurgical coal, with 85 per cent of our production in Alberta and British Columbia.... Preliminary numbers from Natural Resources Canada show that total value of Canada's coal production increased 55.6 per cent to reach $6.3-billion in 2017 as a result of higher prices for the second year in a row....

"While B.C. is the powerhouse producer of metallurgical coal in Canada ... Alberta's production will increase in the coming years. It is no secret that Alberta's foothills and Eastern Slopes hold major deposits of high-quality coking coal, and several projects are moving towards production."

The company everyone is watching is Benga Mining (a wholly owned subsidiary of Australia-based Riversdale

Resources). Should the company's Grassy Mountain project survive a joint federal–provincial environmental review currently underway, the company plans to open a 2800-hectare mountaintop removal mine north of Blairmore by 2021.

Other companies are waiting to see how Riversdale does with the Grassy Mountain approval before advancing mine development plans of their own. Montem Resources hopes to reopen another abandoned mine in the area and has leased an incredible 220 km^2 stretching well north into undeveloped terrain. Max Wang, CEO of Montem's predecessor company, Atrum, was quoted in a recent *Calgary Herald* story: "I would say the industry is looking to the success of Riversdale's project, because it's the first in the Crowsnest Pass area. There are quite a number of global investors, mostly from Australia, interested in that region."

The proposed new Grassy Mountain coal mine falls almost entirely in the Municipal District of Ranchland, but Cam Gardner only learned about the mining plans through a story in a Crowsnest Pass newspaper. At that point, Riversdale Resources had already spent several months grooming the neighbouring MD of Crowsnest Pass, making donations to popular local causes and getting company staff appointed to volunteer boards.

Gardner, who stepped down as reeve of the MD of Ranchland in early 2019 to run as the NDP candidate for Livingstone-Macleod, ranches in an isolated valley west of Chain Lakes Provincial Park, an hour's drive north of the pass. It should be a paradise, but coal is already breathing down his family's neck. Gardner says that they regularly hear explosions from the Fording River mines owned by Teck Resources, 40 km to the west in BC. Montem's undeveloped leases adjacent to Alberta's Forestry Trunk Road (Highway 940) are even closer.

At night, the glow from the BC mines is brighter than the glow from Calgary. "Teck took away our Northern Lights," Gardner says.

"Crowsnest Pass has almost made the transition out of a boom and bust resource economy," Gardner continues, shaking his head over the degree to which some locals have become mine boosters. "They've gone through all the pain of watching the big resource companies shut down to the point where they almost are where Banff and Waterton are, and now they just want to go back to boom and bust."

While Crowsnest Pass flirts with a return to its polluted past, other former coal mining communities have found prosperity by embracing the more pristine attractions of nature. Like the Crowsnest Pass, Canmore also began as a coal-mining town. Its last mine closed in 1979. By the early 1980s it was a struggling backwater. After the 1988 Winter Olympics brought the world to the Alberta Rockies, however, the town blossomed as a tourism and second-home mecca at the doorstep of Banff National Park. Gardner and others see its thriving economy as an example for the Crowsnest Pass if it were to embrace its proximity to the new Castle Provincial Park and other nearby protected areas rather than once again succumbing to the seduction of King Coal.

The coal always runs out, after all. Investors pocket their profits and move on. Towns are left in crisis, the land with open wounds. And coal mining doesn't even put a lot of money in the province's treasury to help mitigate those consequences. Annual royalties from all of Alberta's metallurgical coal mines amounted to barely $5 million in 2018.

If the world's continuing hunger for metallurgical coal leads to a coal mining renaissance along the front of the Rockies, what will that mean for the rest of the ecological sandwich wrapped around those coal seams?

Whereas many biologists turn up their noses at reclaimed coal mines, Beth MacCallum adopts a more pragmatic – even optimistic – view about the implications of ripping the top off the coal sandwich. She's worked on reconciling mining with wildlife since she first arrived in Hinton in 1985. When MacCallum started working on the area's coal mines, government was promoting better reclamation standards for strip mines but had little experience in achieving them. She's seen enough evolution in practice to now believe that reclamation can restore ecosystem values even if it can't restore aesthetics. Since Teck Resources closed the Gregg River and Luscar mines in 2000 and 2003, respectively, she's provided wildlife habitat advice to help the company gain certification of their cleanup efforts.

Some of the world's largest bighorn sheep occupy those mines. Early reclamation efforts focused on simply getting green vegetation growing, so the mine managers planted tame pasture mixes that included a lot of alfalfa and clover. The reclaimed sites became giant salad bars, custom-made for bighorns. The world-record hunter-killed bighorn ram, until recently, was shot just outside the mine boundary. Each fall, hopeful hunters wait for the next massive ram to step across the line and into the record books.

Planting tame hay doesn't replace the ecological diversity lost when land is stripped for mining. But MacCallum says that good mine planning and continuing improvements in reclamation techniques can get partway there. The key, she says, is to stockpile the bulldozed soil for as short a time as possible before spreading it on reclaimed ground. If rain doesn't wash away the soil, the still-viable seeds and root fragments of native grasses, wildflowers and shrubs can resprout. Mines that continually reclaim behind them as they open new seams can move freshly disturbed ground onto newly reclaimed slopes. They still end up with too many weeds and non-native grasses, but there is far more natural diversity than the old-style reclamation that makes trophy hunters happy.

The Luscar and Gregg River mines may soon be certified as fully reclaimed, at which point Teck Resources will hand the land back to the Alberta government. MacCallum says that wolves are already denning on the mine property and it has one of the highest densities of grizzly bears north of the North Saskatchewan River. Marmots are abundant, as are their predators. In fact, she says, most of the original native fauna now thrive on the reclaimed lands. Some wildlife guides even bring clients to the mines instead of nearby Jasper National Park.

There's better wildlife viewing there. That, and the potential for displacement of habituated wildlife by hunters and photographers, is why MacCallum hopes the reclaimed mines will continue being managed as wildlife sanctuaries.

Other problems, however, are more intractable. Perhaps the most troubling is the release of toxic chemicals from the billions of tons of shattered rock that accumulate during the life of a mine. Snowmelt and rainwaters leach sulphates, nitrates and heavy metals like arsenic, cadmium and selenium into groundwater and streams for decades.

Teck Resources operates five coal strip mines in the Elk River valley, just across the Continental Divide from the Alberta deposits currently being eyed by Riversdale and Montum. Selenium pollution from those mines has caused fish kills, deformities and spawning failures in the Elk and Fording rivers. A 2013 University of Montana study documented selenium concentrations seven to ten times higher than natural levels. That triggered a review by the International Joint Commission (IJC) that mediates transboundary water issues between the US and Canada. Federal fisheries officials in Canada became concerned when native cutthroat trout in the Fording River started showing deformities.

Faced with the risk of limitations on its future

expansion plans, in 2014 Teck Resources committed more than $600 million to efforts to reduce selenium pollution. One of its first efforts was to build a cutting-edge bio-remediation facility at Fording River. Soon after it went into operation, however, large numbers of dead trout appeared in the river. The plant was shut down and subsequent analysis showed that, in removing one selenium compound from the water, the plant was actually releasing a more dangerous version of the toxin. The federal Department of Fisheries and Oceans fined the company $1,425,000. The plant remains closed. The problem seems insoluble – but Teck still hopes to expand.

"There is a question as to whether the technology even exists to remove selenium from large volumes of flowing water and there is no viable solution to remove selenium from groundwater," US commissioners to the IJC wrote in a 2018 report.

And Teck's selenium problems aren't just confined to BC. Monitoring downstream from the Hinton-area mines in creeks containing the rare and threatened Athabasca rainbow trout has shown levels of selenium contamination two to four times higher than federal guidelines for the protection of aquatic life. Although Teck reports no evidence of harm to the trout, fisheries biologist Carl

Hunt points out that evidence of mortality is always hard to find in the wild because selenium is most toxic to eggs and young fish. Compounding the problem: selenium is more toxic to native rainbow trout than to the introduced eastern brook trout – a species that tends to out-compete our native trout at the best of times.

Farther south, in the Oldman River headwaters, Alberta will soon have to decide whether to allow Australian-owned mining companies Riversdale and Montem to open new mines on leases that cover an area almost as large as the Elk valley mines. Such approvals would almost certainly inflict water pollution on downstream ecosystems and water users: our streams are small, water is scarce, and the wind blows much more strongly than on the BC side of the mountains. Pollution will likely be more concentrated in streams, and more widely dispersed on land.

Rancher Jillian Lawson pointed out the intractability of the problem during a joint federal–provincial panel review of the Grassy Mountain project. Noting that the proposed mine would rely merely on settling ponds and rock filtration to treat water before releasing it into streams containing westslope cutthroat trout – a nationally designated species at risk – she added: "The dust and fly ash from the proposed mine(s) would be blown far and wide, especially in the prevailing – and increasingly extreme – southwest winds to contaminate other sources of water including the snow pack on the mountains ... where it could make its way to ground water which recharges domestic wells and essential natural springs."

Fisheries biologist Lorne Fitch says that native cutthroat trout are already extirpated from 80 per cent of their historic range in Alberta. Some of their last productive habitat is the streams draining the coal deposits Riversdale and Montem hope to develop. There's little likelihood that those streams will survive mountaintop-removal mining. Even if some do, chances are that non-native fishes more resistant to pollution will replace the unique native cutthroats and bull trout.

In a 2005 *Alberta Views* essay about the Cheviot mine, geologist Ben Gadd wrote: "Alberta's mining industry is capable of overcoming any opposition and spoiling any place it wishes, including lands as beautiful and ecologically important as Mountain Park. Our province needs a government able to enact truly protective laws and willing to enforce them. It needs regulators with backbone."[1]

If the next metallurgical coal boom leads to massive new

mines in the headwaters of Alberta's Oldman River, the beauty of that country will be impaired forever. Bighorn sheep and the other wildlife with which they share the high, windy slopes will likely persist, albeit in strangely artificial, man-made habitats. Streams will still flow east to the thirsty plains, but devoid of native trout and loaded up with toxic chemicals.

And somewhere else in the world, that Alberta coal will be combusted, releasing hundreds of millions more tons of carbon dioxide into the planet's warming atmosphere. But the foreign investors feasting on Alberta's coal sandwich will have made some money.

3

THE COST OF OIL

PIPE DREAMS

Alberta sometimes seems tone-deaf on climate change and single-mindedly obsessed with the sacred mission of selling bitumen to the world. It sometimes seems like we've forgotten that this province is more than its hydrocarbons.

Oil and gas have been generous, if fickle, friends. When prices peak, we get briefly rich. Soon we're convinced we'll be rich forever. Then when prices tank, as resource prices always do, we get cranky and look for someone to blame.

When OPEC flooded the market with cheap oil in the 1980s, we blamed Pierre Elliott Trudeau and his National Energy Program. When Saudi Arabia more recently undercut oil prices again, many Albertans chose to blame Trudeau's son and Alberta's newly elected government. Their sin? They took too long approving a new pipeline.

Don't look for logic in that position. Just as critics ignore the law of supply and demand, they don't explain how a new pipeline will help Alberta sell crude whose production costs $80 or more per barrel when customers can buy it from other producers for under $50. The urgency with which pundits, politicians and petro-partisans clamour for new pipelines might make one wonder if anybody studies economics anymore.

But the blame and finger pointing about pipelines is not, ultimately, about Alberta's future. It's the politics of nostalgia and denial, and it's both stupid and irresponsible.

Oil, gas and coal are marvellous energy sources. Instead of relying on the energy available on the surface of the planet in any given year, our exploitation of hydrocarbon fuels allows us to use energy that took millennia to accumulate in prehistoric swamps and oceans. In barely a century we've already burned through hundreds of thousands of years' worth of energy. In doing so, however, we released massive stores of carbon into the atmosphere as carbon dioxide.

In 2016, for the first time, scientists recorded 400 ppm (parts per million) of carbon dioxide in Earth's atmosphere – 40 per cent more than at the start of the Industrial Revolution. Carbon dioxide – and more potent greenhouse gases like methane, also released by the hydrocarbon economy – is to a planet what glass is to a greenhouse. Adding layers of glass to a greenhouse holds in more heat and extends the growing season – but it can also kill the whole crop if excess heat isn't vented.

Earth has no vents from which to release heat. All the extra greenhouse gases in our atmosphere simply hold it in. That heat doesn't just change regional climates – its energy creates storms and winds of unprecedented intensity.

The nostalgia of those who drank the heady wine of Alberta's oil booms is understandable. The purr of a new pickup truck, the smell of new furniture in a new home, those great vacations on sunny beaches in mid-winter – all that prosperity; didn't we earn it, after all?

No, we didn't. We were lucky. And we squandered our luck. We elected governments that catered to greed by cutting taxes and writing off the environment. Rather than pay sales tax like other, lesser, mortals we relied on oil revenues to cover government operating costs or simply put off essential investments in public infrastructure and services. We believed the good times would last forever because that's what we wanted to believe. When, inevitably, they didn't, we were offended by Jim Prentice's suggestion that we look in the mirror for the cause of Alberta's economic malaise. Instead, we opted to blame politicians, bureaucrats and Indigenous communities we saw as standing between Alberta and its next pipeline.

Easy, but wrong. That next pipeline won't save us – because it won't solve the real problem.

The real problem is the climate change juggernaut unleashed by our addiction to carbon fuels.

That problem is evident in unprecedented forest droughts yielding increasingly frequent and more severe wildfires and insect outbreaks. It shows in "100-year floods" that now come every decade or so and, ironically, summer water shortages along the same rivers. It shows in extreme weather events, once rare, that have become normal – driving unprecedented disaster insurance costs. Warm-climate pestilences like Lyme disease, West Nile virus and whirling disease, previously unknown here, are also symptoms of the problem.

The costs of climate change are mounting, but we seem reluctant to abandon the fantasy that oil can be as much a part of our future as of our past. Our denial may well lead to other regions of the world leaping ahead of us in developing renewable energy production systems and storage technologies.

Alberta can neither afford the costs of climate change nor sustain our economy on the carbon fuels that drive it. New pipelines, should they come, will simply perpetuate our hopeless addiction to a doomed and destructive energy source.

What an irony, if future Albertans get stuck paying for empty pipelines while also having to buy renewable energy supplies from others who developed them while this generation was lost in a pipe dream.

THE PIPELINES WE NEED

Read any of Alberta's daily newspapers and you will know that our province's only hope is new pipelines. Nothing else will save us. I took some convincing, but I'm in. In fact, I'd like to propose two new pipelines.

These pipelines, unlike Trans Mountain or the thankfully dead Northern Gateway, should be less controversial. As water pipelines, they shouldn't require environmental double-speak and weird rationalizations about "ethical oil" and how pumping more bitumen will reduce greenhouse emissions. If they leak, that's just a duck pond. People like ducks, at least live ones.

One of my proposed pipelines would draw water from the delta of the Peace and Athabasca rivers in Wood Buffalo National Park. Its purpose: to provide drinking water to towns and cities from, say, Red Deer north. The other would draw water from the South Saskatchewan River near Empress, downstream of Medicine Hat, to southern Alberta communities. They would replace existing water sources.

The farther downstream one goes, the bigger the river, right? So these two pipelines should deliver more than enough water for the future needs of our province.

Well, maybe not that southern pipeline. The South Saskatchewan carries the combined flows of the Bow and Oldman rivers. But a 2009 government study found that before the river crosses the border, more than half of its summer flow is sucked out to irrigate crops. The World Wildlife Fund says that up to 90 per cent of the Bow River's flow goes to farms some years. At times it's possible to walk across the river near Bassano and barely wet your knees – try that in Calgary.

That water grows potatoes for potato chips, sugar beets for sugar and forage crops for cattle. Irrigation proponents often insist their crops are feeding a hungry world. But irrigation, like any other industry, is driven by profit margins. The hungry people of the world can't afford most irrigation crops.

Replacing existing wells and dams with a pipeline from the downstream limit of the South Saskatchewan River would force us to rethink how generously we subsidize the fattening of our nation with river water. Irrigation makes sense in that drought-prone area, but only for growing food that's actually needed. A more conservative approach – irrigating for food and not for fat – would leave more water in the rivers. More water in the rivers would also improve water quality. A 2009 study for Alberta Agriculture found that the lower Bow and Oldman rivers have the lowest riparian health values possible and that pesticide loadings exceed levels harmful to fishes and invertebrates.

But there is big money in irrigation; I expect stiff opposition to my pipeline proposal. The northern pipeline proposal will face resistance too. It would draw water from the heart of Wood Buffalo National Park, which is recognized by the United Nations Educational, Scientific and Cultural Organization (UNESCO) as a World Heritage Site. We don't want to ruin world heritage, do we?

Actually we're already ruining it. The BC government permanently impaired the Peace River's flow regime when it built the W.A.C. Bennett Dam in 1968. The Peace–Athabasca delta promptly began to dry out. Engineers tried building weirs in the park to replace the flood flows, but the deterioration continues. BC's Site C dam, now under construction, will make things even worse. Most Albertans live upstream, which is probably why they aren't kicking up a fuss about the price that muskrats, moose, wood bison and small Cree communities will all pay.

They're already paying another price: the Athabasca River is chronically polluted with chemical residues from oil sands mining in Alberta. Fish have tumours, cancer rates are high and the people whose families trusted the river for generations no longer consider its water safe.

A 2017 UNESCO study found that nearly every indicator of well-being for this World Heritage Site is degraded, mostly because upstream abuse sends sick rivers into the delta.

That's why we need the pipeline. If the people of Edmonton and other large communities had to drink that water, you can bet we'd keep it clean. We'd fight hard to keep both those rivers healthy. For now, however, we happily pocket our profits from river abuse, ignoring the plight of the park and its politically powerless Indigenous communities.

Good neighbours don't hog water and flush their problems down the river for the ecosystem and the neighbours to cope with. But we do. We divert upstream waters to our towns and cities, and send shrunken, polluted rivers out of the province. If our drinking water came from the downstream ends of those rivers, we'd be more motivated to keep them well watered and clean. That would make us better neighbours. Actually, it might make us better people.

It's time to lay some pipe.

PERVERSE POLICY

October, for me, used to mean duck hunting: the fecund smell of prairie potholes, a spreading sunrise glow along the eastern horizon and the whistle of mallard wings overhead. Saskatchewan describes itself as "the land of living skies," but that title belongs to pretty much any wetland ecosystem. Long, shifting lines of snow geese shimmer against the sky. Swans and herons fly heavily above the reeds and rushes. Coots creak, ducks quack, small shy sparrows lisp among the willows, and by the time the sun is fully up it seems like the world fairly hums with life.

I don't hunt ducks anymore, but it was only an excuse anyway; I still haunt Alberta's wet places whenever I can.

It's not just about ducks, after all; these are hotbeds of biodiversity. From beaver ponds to prairie sloughs to the boreal forest's sprawling muskeg peatlands, at least 600 species of plants, animals and insects depend on our wetlands. These ecosystems also absorb copious amounts of carbon. One way to reduce the CO_2 in our atmosphere – much of it the result of our burning coal and other hydrocarbons that originated in prehistoric marshes – would be to let nature store it in wetlands.

But for that to happen the wetlands have to be there.

When Alberta became a province, more than one-fifth was wetland. Now, however, the Institute for Wetland and Waterfowl Research calculates that 64 per cent of the sloughs and marshes in the settled areas of the province are gone. That means we've wiped out more than 21,500 km^2 of vital wildlife habitat, along with its ability to store carbon and recharge groundwater. Agriculture and cities account for most of that wetland destruction.

Farther north, oil sands developments are now eating into boreal wetlands that once teemed with sandhill cranes, palm warblers, wood frogs, moose and other native wildlife. According to the Alberta Wilderness Association, northern Alberta contains "about 11 per cent of Canada's peatlands ... representing unique ecosystems that provide habitat for over 400 species of plants, many of them threatened or endangered. Many wildlife species are associated with peatlands as well, including the endangered woodland caribou. The role these vast peat bogs play in climate stability is just beginning to be understood, and this may be their greatest ecological service."

Every wetland in the province belongs to the public –
something many landowners don't know or else prefer
not to acknowledge. If those are our wetlands, our government had better have a plan. And they do. After many
months of analysis and consultation, Alberta's Wetland
Policy was released in 2011. It was intended to end our devastating rate of wetland loss.

Almost a decade later, it's failing to deliver.

The original draft policy prescribed a "no-net-loss"
standard: every acre of wetland damaged by development
would have to be replaced by an acre of the same kind of
wetland elsewhere. Given the massive losses already suffered, this set the bar pretty low. Still, on a go-forward
basis it made sense.

In a paper for Environmental Marketplace, policy analysts Becca Madsen and Hannah Kett describe what then
went wrong. Of 20 interest sectors the government consulted, 18 supported the working draft. Two – the Alberta
Chamber of Resources and the Canadian Association of
Petroleum Producers (CAPP) – were opposed. "These dis-
senters represent economic interest in the development of
the … oil sands," wrote Madsen and Kett. "Both opposed
the policy of 'no-net loss,' [claiming it] would cost billions
and inhibit economic development."

The analysts add, a bit incredulously, that CAPP argued that peatlands are impossible to restore and "would have to be replaced with an alternative wetland restoration/creation [which] 'undermin(es) the ecological rational for the no-net-loss paradigm altogether'.... CAPP is basically telling the people of Alberta that they will lose their wetlands when oil companies develop oil sands (earning billions) and that these oil companies are not going to pay for their restoration."

Perverse logic, but oil rules Alberta; tame politicians approved a wetlands policy that lets developers – especially in the north – simply pay one-time fees rather than actually replace the wetlands they ruin.

Most finalized policies, by the time everyone has had a kick at watering them down, are already weak soup. Implementation then becomes a series of compromises and reinterpretations. In the case of Alberta's wetland policy, the road of least resistance has been to lowball the cost of wetland replacement so that developers face no real financial disincentive from continuing to trash our surviving wetlands. And in the north, toxic tailings ponds grow while peatlands vanish.

CAPP helped turn Alberta's wetlands policy into an oil sands one. Good trick.

OIL SUCKS

I'm an addict. I use oil. We all do. That's how we've wired our economy. But the fact that we're hopelessly hooked doesn't mean we shouldn't confront the issue. The first step, after all, is admitting you have a problem.

Addicts don't make rational choices. They specialize in denial and ignore the harm their addiction causes them and others. They'll sacrifice just about anything or anyone for that next fix. Once they're addicted, the drug owns them. Quitting seems impossible.

Like oil. But if we want to get our health back and make our relationships whole again, we need to kick the habit that keeps us sick.

Recent hysteria over a proposed pipeline to BC illustrates the cost we're willing to pay to sustain our addiction. Regardless of the legitimate worries of our good neighbours in BC – whom we expect to shoulder all the environmental risks should the pipeline fail or a tanker run aground – we seem prepared to tear Confederation apart and poison long-standing relationships as long as the oil keeps flowing. That's addict behaviour, not the behaviour of people who care about others.

Addicts don't just ignore the harm their compulsions cause to friends and family. They ignore their own well-being.

Alberta has over 320,000 km of unreclaimed seismic lines riddling our landscape with erosion scars that choke streams and reservoirs with silt. Over 330,000 oil and gas wells penetrate our drinking water aquifers and leak methane into the atmosphere. More than 384,000 km of pipelines are slowly deteriorating underground. The oil sands region has over 220 km^2 of toxic tailings ponds; nobody has a viable plan for reclaiming them even though they already contaminate the region's waters.

Oil industry flacks get paid to jump on statements like these with reassurances that wells and tailings ponds don't leak and industry's environmental performance is improving. When it comes to glib assurances, Big Oil can out-tobacco Big Tobacco – another industry that profits from addiction. But guess what: cigarettes do, indeed, cause cancer and heart disease. And methane does, in fact, leak from oil and gas wells. And those tumours in fish downstream from Fort McMurray are not actually natural.

Some will consider this blasphemy, coming from a fourth-generation Albertan. Looking back over those generations, however, I don't see many oil jobs. My family has worked mostly in other sectors of the economy. That shouldn't be surprising: there are actually other ways of making a living in Alberta. Farming and ranching come to mind. Installing wind and solar generation. Forestry, tourism, education, medicine, manufacturing, writing (well, maybe not writing).... the list goes on. But from the chatter in the opium den, you'd think oil was our only truth. Here's a truth: the Alberta government actually collects more money from our other addictions – alcohol and gambling – than from oil and gas royalties. That's because, after more than 20 cuts to royalty rates, oil and gas companies now pocket our share of petroleum profits. But as addicts, we'll settle for crumbs as long as oil flows.

Oil interests usually cheerlead for free-enterprise capitalism and small government and, eager to support the dealers of their opiate, many Albertans do the same. But most of the oil industry is pure socialism; capitalism only shows up on one side of the ledger. Most oil companies are capitalists where profits are concerned, but dedicated socialists with regard to risks, research expenses and environmental costs. We taxpayers paid for the university research that made oil sands production possible. Taxpayers now not only finance public relations programs for pipeline companies but assume industry risks by buying lines outright and building them. Having socialized their own responsibilities, the oil industry shamelessly cajoled a series of so-called conservative governments into reducing royalties; we now keep barely more than one loonie for every $100 of profit from the sale of our own bitumen. The Alberta Energy Regulator estimates it will cost more than $260 billion to clean up the industry's environmental messes. There's nowhere near that amount of money in public coffers to cover that cost. But addicts don't worry about tomorrow; they just want their next hit.

You read it here first: no oil company will ever reclaim the oil sands sludge ponds. That liability will be entirely socialized (dumped on government) by the so-called capitalists. Our money will be long gone, the oil will no longer flow, and we'll be stuck with the muck. That's how things end up for addicts.

And I haven't even mentioned the impacts and costs of climate change.

An addict doesn't want to face reality; he or she just wants to know there will be a next fix. There will be. We're already in that fix. Oil sucks. And we're the suckers.

TROUBLED GROUNDWATERS

We didn't hike on trails to our fishing streams back in the 1960s. We followed cutlines. There were more of them every year. Oil companies would set off explosives along the bulldozed lines and use the seismic echoes to map the underlying rocks.

It was along one such cutline that I encountered my first artesian spring. Dad stopped abruptly to keep from stepping into a marsh that had not been there two weeks earlier. Water had spread across the cutline from a growing pool in the forest. A small fountain burbled out of one corner.

"Where's that water coming from?" I asked. I was thinking about Yellowstone and geysers. "The seismic crew must have opened up an artesian spring," Dad replied. "It's underground water coming up."

By the following summer our cutline was blocked by a small lake full of dead trees.

Dad couldn't tell me where that newly freed groundwater originated. He didn't know. The drilling crew didn't know either. The government didn't know. It's entirely possible we still don't know.

We should. Groundwater is going to be a lot more important in our future than it was in my childhood. Out of sight and too often out of mind, underground aquifers keep rivers flowing, provide drinkable water, irrigate farm gardens and feedlots and provide injection water for extracting oil and natural gas. Almost a quarter of Alberta's population relies on wells for their drinking water, including up to 90 per cent of rural residents. We treat this hidden supply as if it will always be abundant, pure and available.

It may not be. As Alberta begins to depend more and more on groundwater, we need to keep better track of how much we're using, how well the supply is being renewed and the extent to which leaking oil and gas wells, fracking and surface pollution are depleting and contaminating this vital resource down below. We know far less about Alberta's groundwater than we need to, even though almost everything we do affects its abundance, quality and availability.

Compared to most other Canadian provinces, Alberta is water-scarce, especially in the southern half, where most of us live. River flows have been declining – the combined natural flow of the Bow and Oldman rivers has diminished to about 90 per cent of what it was half a century ago – even as the region's population has tripled. Two-thirds of Canada's irrigated agriculture, a major water consumer, is in the Bow and Oldman basins. Farther north, oil sands extraction has become a major water consumer; it may eventually permanently remove more than a tenth of the Athabasca River's flow.

Water security may be Alberta's biggest long-term challenge – economic, social and environmental. In 2003, after many years of reacting to various challenges as they arose, the Alberta government moved to a more proactive stance with its Water for Life strategy, which aims to provide Albertans with a safe, secure drinking water supply and healthy aquatic ecosystems while ensuring that scarcity of this precious resource doesn't limit our economic well-being.

Most of Alberta's water has traditionally been drawn from streams and lakes. The stuff on the surface is easy to find and develop. It's also well mapped and easily measured. It's only in recent decades that wells have become an important part of our water supply. Groundwater records, consequently, rarely extend back beyond the 1960s.

University of Saskatchewan researcher Cesar Perez-Valdivia found a way to extend the local record farther into the past. He analyzed 33 groundwater wells across the prairie provinces and then cross-correlated their records with tree-ring chronologies to trace changes over 300 years. He found that Alberta's groundwater levels have been stable or gradually declining in most regions.

A model developed for Alberta Environment and Parks estimates that, in an average year, almost six million Olympic-sized swimming pools of water drain into Alberta's aquifers and the equivalent amount drains out of them into rivers and lakes. That's a simplified picture; the amount varies each year with precipitation and evaporation rates, which are not the same from one part of the province to another.

Along the gravel-bed rivers that drain the eastern slopes of the Rocky Mountains, groundwater is constantly welling up to become river water, and river water is draining through the stream bed to become groundwater. Calgary researchers Leanne Cantafio and Cathryn Ryan studied the Elbow River in Calgary and found that, every second of the day, 20 litres of water per kilometre moves from the river into the ground or back again.

Deeper bedrock aquifers are the most abundant, and least understood, of Alberta's groundwater resources. The artesian spring that the seismic crew released near our secret trout stream all those years ago was likely from a confined bedrock aquifer.

In 2006, to put more meat on the bones of its Water for Life strategy, Alberta Environment asked the Rosenberg International Forum on Water Policy for advice. Based at the University of California, the biennial forum brings scientists and policymakers together to create smart guidelines. The Rosenberg Forum assembled an expert panel to review Alberta's water management, identify weaknesses and make recommendations to strengthen it. Government officials specifically asked the panel to review Alberta's groundwater management and suggest improvements.

Their 2007 report recommended that surface watersheds and aquifer systems be considered together when managing either, because of the intimate connections between water recharge from the land and water transfer through aquifers. It also identified a critical weakness: a lack of good monitoring programs and inventories of groundwater aquifers and the demands being placed on them. "Previous practices of groundwater monitoring and management," the Rosenberg report's authors wrote, "were appropriate to an era in which groundwater was a relatively minor source of supply in most areas. These practices will not be adequate in an era of intensifying pressure to develop groundwater resources."

A year later, Alberta launched its first Provincial Groundwater Inventory Program. Coordinated jointly by Alberta Environment and Parks and the Alberta Geological Survey, the program aims to map and measure fresh groundwater supplies across the province.

The only such inventory completed to date is the Edmonton–Calgary Corridor Groundwater Atlas (2011), which describes all the usable groundwater resources in a 49,500 km^2 area centred on the Highway 2 corridor between Calgary and Edmonton. As other regional inventories are completed, the government will finally be able to identify critical recharge areas that need to be protected and to predict how much water can safely be withdrawn from various aquifers.

As Alberta plays catch-up with inventory and analysis, our ability to anticipate and avoid water security challenges will improve. In some cases, though, the horse is already out of the barn. We are already dealing with serious challenges: depletion of local aquifers, loss of groundwater recharge and contamination of those precious hidden reservoirs.

Big cities such as Edmonton, Red Deer, Calgary and Lethbridge quench their thirst by drawing from rivers, but many smaller communities rely on wells. Banff, Canmore and Okotoks pump groundwater from wells drilled into alluvial aquifers beneath their local rivers. Other towns, such as St. Albert, Stony Plain, Bon Accord, Westlock and Vermilion, draw from aquifers that originate largely as rain and snowmelt draining into local hill systems and wetlands.

Even where a town's supply is closely tied to a river, it can be limited. The entire surface water supply of the Bow and Oldman drainages has already been allocated to current and future uses; as a result, the province has had a moratorium on new water licences in the basin since 2006. It's not just the rivers that are tapped out; the surface zones of their associated alluvial aquifers are too. That's why Okotoks was caught in a region-wide freeze on new water licences; any further pumping would actually start drawing down the Sheep River. The town plans to pipe water in from Calgary for future needs.

And even where groundwater supplies are recharged only by a region's precipitation and don't affect the flow of nearby streams, aquifers can get badly depleted. The town of Irricana got a licence in the early 1980s to draw from an aquifer that regulators assumed would easily meet a growing population's needs. By 2005 the level in the town well had dropped 12 metres; the aquifer was sucked nearly dry. The town ceased pumping and instead built a pipeline to bring treated river water in from Drumheller. A decade later, Irricana's groundwater well is still more than four metres below its original level.

Masaki Hayashi likens groundwater to a chequing account. A physical hydrologist at the University of Calgary, Hayashi says that as surface water supplies become increasingly taxed, Alberta is going to start making bigger withdrawals from its aquifers. If we take water out faster than the aquifer refills, the balance drops and eventually we end up overdrawn. Unlike a real bank, however, aquifers don't offer overdraft protection.

There are two possible reasons for a shrinking bank account: too many withdrawals or not enough deposits. Where groundwater is concerned, depositing less is clearly a bad idea. But that is what is happening with some of Alberta's aquifers.

Groundwater originates as snowmelt and rain. It gets recharged pretty much anywhere that surface water goes into the ground, but areas of lush vegetation and porous soils are particularly important for moving surface water into aquifers. Land uses that increase runoff – such as compacting the soil under roads and urban development or breaking up vegetation cover with clear-cut logging, off-road recreation or heavy livestock grazing – reduce the amount of water deposited into Alberta's underground accounts each year.

University of Calgary geohydrologist Cathy Ryan has taken a special interest in the Elbow River, which she describes as the only river in the world whose primary end use is to provide municipal water for a large city. Her research program has shown that almost all the flow in the Elbow originates in the Rocky Mountains. The entire alluvial aquifer under that river, and other connected aquifers, depends on a porous, well-vegetated landscape upstream from Bragg Creek. Industrial-scale logging and a network of hardened roads and off-highway vehicle trails, however, divert much of the potential groundwater recharge overland into the river each spring. Instead of replenishing aquifers, the lost runoff feeds increasingly severe river floods.

Farther north, in a 2009 report for the North Saskatchewan Watershed Alliance, Morris Maccagno and João Küpper came to a similar conclusion. They believe that land-use decisions that reduce groundwater recharge could dry up the North Saskatchewan drainage's most important alluvial and bedrock aquifers. "The dynamics of regional groundwater recharge in the Rocky Mountains and Foothills," they wrote, "should be characterized in terms of contributions to baseflow in the headwaters and to regional flow in the Paskapoo aquifer system, as well as the sensitivities of regional groundwater flow to the effects of forestry practices, land-use change and climate change in the headwaters."

Hayashi stresses, however, that land use in the forested headwaters of Alberta's major rivers has little impact on most Alberta water wells. Most farm and town wells across central and eastern Alberta draw from shallow aquifers whose recharge areas are less than 100 km away. Mapping, and then protecting, those critical recharge areas is essential because these small, localized aquifers have little ability to buffer any loss in supply. They are also more vulnerable to pollution.

When most Albertans hear about water pollution, we tend to think of the oil sands region northeast of Edmonton. Groundwater pollution is indeed a growing problem there. The water table is very near the surface across much of the Athabasca drainage; it's difficult to dig a pit without encountering water that connects underground to nearby lakes, rivers, wetlands and aquifers. Toxic wastes abound in the region's nearly 200 km^2 of tailings ponds. Modelling studies have estimated that as much as 6.5 million litres can leak daily from some of those ponds. While most contamination studies have focused on the Athabasca River, the polluted flow moves continually in and out of adjacent aquifers.

But groundwater contamination from the petroleum industry is a far bigger problem than just keeping toxic oil sands extraction by-products out of boreal rivers. That artesian spring that Dad and we kids stumbled across five decades ago was merely the tip of the iceberg; groundwater damage may be widespread. If so, we won't necessarily hear about it from industry, government regulators or even the private citizens whose wells have been contaminated.

Alberta has been drilling holes through its aquifers for over a century. Almost half a million oil and natural gas wells spike the landscape now, according to records maintained by the Alberta Energy Regulator (AER), a government body funded entirely by the oil and gas industry it was set up to regulate. About a third no longer produce oil or gas. When a well becomes inactive, the company is supposed to "abandon" it (i.e., decommission it) according to strict industry protocols.

Well operators have to submit an abandonment plan and check on the condition of any cement in the well. They then clean petroleum residues from the pipe, block any escaping methane gas, seal off groundwater zones with cement and cap the well. The theory is that the metal pipe, filled with cement down to a level below any potable groundwater, protects aquifers. In reality, even if the original well didn't contaminate an aquifer with drilling or fracking fluids or through methane leakage along the well bore, abandoned wells can be plagued by pipe corrosion, cement failure or damage from industry's increasingly common practice of inducing subterranean earthquakes to release oil and gas trapped in relatively impermeable rock formations. Fracking, as it's called, deliberately shatters underground rock. Although most fracking is done far beneath freshwater aquifers, it's still risky, considering that aquifers are best protected by intact rock layers.

The AER has a history of downplaying the risks associated with oil and gas extraction and well abandonment. The agency stubbornly insists that no drinking water well has ever been contaminated by a petroleum well in Alberta, but concedes on its website: "While abandoned wells do not place the environment or public at significant risk, small leaks are possible. A well leak can be caused by many things, including corrosion, improper abandonment and damage incurred during excavation." Research has shown that fracking can cause leaks in nearby wells too.

Once the AER approves a well remediation plan, the company has to repair any ensuing leaks. That's the theory. But when companies get into financial trouble, the orderly well-abandonment process can fall apart. Many companies simply walk away from unreclaimed or leaking wells. When that happens, the AER requires Alberta's industry-funded Orphan Well Association to shut the wells in. The association, however, has a backlog of more than 700 unreclaimed wells, any or all of which could be contaminating groundwater. It can cost millions of dollars to reclaim one well; that's partly why the association has only reclaimed about 30 a year since its predecessor's inception in 1994.

According to one recent summary, Alberta has about 80,000 inactive wells outside the orphan well program.

While most of those have been decommissioned according to the prescribed protocol, about 37,000 are out of compliance with AER requirements. In addition, at least 13,500 are ticking time bombs that have yet to be properly remediated.

Some landowners and politicians have called for the Alberta government to use public money to remediate orphaned wells during the current economic recession, arguing that, among other things, such a program would keep drilling contractors working until demand for new oil and gas wells picks up again. The government has resisted that idea, citing Alberta's long-standing polluter-pay principle and the risks of allowing industry to transfer its environmental liabilities onto taxpayers. Even if the government were willing to entertain the idea, little public money is available due to the practice in Alberta, over the past two decades, of charging bargain-basement royalties in order to keep those now-failing companies in business.[2]

Without a greater sense of urgency and more aggressive levies on industry, there is little prospect that many of Alberta's abandoned wells will ever be properly sealed. Once the consequences of that failure turn up in our drinking water wells, it will be too late. It is far easier to pollute groundwater than to clean it up again.

However, it's not just energy wells that expose ground-water to the risk of contamination. Alberta is littered with tens of thousands of abandoned water wells – potentially an even bigger threat, since they can channel surface contaminants such as septic waste, cattle manure or pesticides directly into aquifers. Some have been safely plugged and capped; others haven't. No regulatory agency checks on this.

Adèle Hurley directs the water issues program for the Munk School of Global Affairs & Public Policy. In a recent *Globe and Mail* editorial she decried the degree to which groundwater contamination is hidden behind legal "non-disclosure" agreements that landowners are forced to sign before oil and gas drilling companies will replace contaminated water wells. Even without such agreements, she says, the public is told next to nothing about contamination of our hidden drinking water supplies by an industry based on punching holes through them.

"To date, no regulatory body in Canada has set up a rigorous program to track methane and other contaminants ... in areas of intense hydrocarbon drilling," she writes. "Yet science shows us that all oil and gas well casings leak over time and … serve as pathways for contaminants that can put groundwater at risk for thousands of years."

Hurley supports a call by David McLaughlin, former head of the National Round Table on the Environment and the Economy, for provincial governments to charge a royalty or fee for groundwater use and allocate the revenues to independent groundwater authorities for mapping and monitoring programs. "Investment in the protection of groundwater," argues Hurley, "is a form of national security."

Alberta will survive when the oil and gas run out. But nothing can survive without water. It's time we defend our groundwater as aggressively as we have become accustomed to protecting those land uses and industries that put our aquifers most at risk.

4

AGRICULTURE

EATING SOIL

Look at a satellite image of Alberta at night, and you can map our richest agricultural soils by the concentration of urban lights. When European immigrants arrived here in the late 19th and early 20th centuries, they were looking for good soil. Our larger towns and cities sprang up in the heart of our best farmland. The cities are still there; increasingly, the soil isn't.

Fescue grassland produced Alberta's finest black soils; that's why fescue grassland is now one of the province's scarcest natural ecosystems. From Lloydminster west to Edmonton, then south through Red Deer to Calgary and a bit beyond, fescue prairie went under the plow while towns and cities grew up to serve the farmers.

Plowing native grassland starved the soil by killing the vegetation whose roots sustained and renewed its organic matter. But prairie agriculture has come some way toward restoring the ecological processes that help soil renew itself. There's always hope for soil as long as there's a place for vegetation to grow. There is no hope, however, once asphalt, strip malls and houses take over.

That's the dark side of the bright arc of light smeared across the face of Alberta each night. That glow illuminates a province that is killing its best farmland. Black prairie soil is piled, even today, on the outskirts of Wainwright, Edmonton, Red Deer, Airdrie, Calgary and most other large towns or cities as urban developers scrape away once-fecund prairie soils and replace them with urban sprawl.

The Alberta Land Institute, based at the University of Alberta, recently released some disturbing statistics about the rate at which we are cannibalizing our best farmland. *Economic Evaluation of Farmland Conversion and Fragmentation in Alberta* found that, in the 30 years ending in 2013, more than 1600 km^2 of land between Calgary and Edmonton was converted to urban or industrial use. That's an area bigger than both cities combined.

Towns and cities don't need to devour more land. They can grow denser. The population density of Edmonton is barely more than 3,000 people per square mile. By contrast, New York City has 27,000 souls per square mile – nine times denser than Edmonton. Vancouver, squeezed as it is between the mountains and the sea, is five times as dense as Alberta's capital.

But Alberta cities aren't constrained by geography – or good policy. That's why most urban Albertans live in mass-produced neighbourhoods that used to be farmland.

Arguably, not everything about sprawl is bad. Demographia, a US think tank, argues that suburban development keeps housing affordable. Their International Housing Affordability Survey analyzed cities around the world and concluded that policies designed to keep cities compact also drive home prices out of reach. But critics counter that the sticker price is only one factor in a home's affordability. Suburban homes often impose long commutes to work and school on their occupants. Transportation and other costs considerably change the affordability equation. Having briefly lived in Okotoks while working in downtown Calgary, I can attest to that; our mortgage seemed affordable, but we barely made it from one paycheque to the next.

Suburbs are a 20th-century aberration built around the private automobile. Fundamentally, suburban sprawl is unsustainable because it consumes non-renewable resources: oil, soil and space. It also hurts community by separating families from the places where they work, go to school, shop and play. Jane Jacobs considered suburbs city killers. They are farm killers too.

Sprawl extends even beyond the suburbs; in recent decades urbanites have been buying land an hour or two out of town to build their homes there. The attraction of "rurban" life is obvious, but if suburbia wastes land and resources, rurbanization is even more extravagant.

Ecologist Brad Stelfox models future changes to the Alberta landscape using various spatial databases and statistics about social, environmental and industry trends. His ALCES model (A Landscape Cumulative Effects Simulator) is used by industry and government to evaluate future investment or policy choices. It should come as no surprise that ALCES predicts ongoing losses of farmland and natural habitats. But what might be surprising is that the biggest culprit isn't suburbia, oil and gas, forestry, mining or another industrial use. It's city people moving to the countryside. Unfortunately, areas near major cities contain not just our most productive agricultural soils; some of Alberta's richest wildlife habitats are in the near-urban foothills, lake country and river valleys.

The 21st century is shaping up to be a time when humanity can no longer avoid hard choices. One of those choices will be whether we consider farmland soils and rural nature as important as the houses and shopping malls with which we're replacing them.

A CLEAN WINDSHIELD

Last summer I drove to The Pas, Manitoba, to visit my daughter. The long, hot drive went through Lethbridge, Medicine Hat and Saskatoon, the heart of prairie Canada. In part I followed the route my great-great-uncle walked back in 1875 from what is now the Wnnipeg area to the St. Paul mission in what is now Alberta.

It was the same route, but a very different prairie.

Leonard Van Tighem was a young seminarian when he crossed the Great Plains to join the Oblate missionaries in the North-West Territories of Canada. He was plagued by mosquitoes and horseflies, flushed grasshoppers and moths out of the prairie wool, heard the wolf-whistle calls of upland sandpipers and the eerie cries of curlews, and saw herds of bison and pronghorns. Overhead, where hawks and cranes circled, the thin swirling song of pipits and tumbling melody of horned larks would have drifted down from the prairie sky. Everywhere: grass, sage and wildflowers.

But he believed in the frontier enterprise of taming the wild. Although he became a staunch advocate for the Piikanii and Kainai people who, after signing Treaty Seven in good faith, were repeatedly betrayed by the Ottawa government and their Indian agents, he probably saw their suffering as an unfortunate cost of the inevitable march of progress. Given that, I imagine my ancestor might have looked at the modern prairie landscape I traversed 143 years later with a certain degree of approval. Because progress had clearly happened.

I, on the other hand, arrived at The Pas in a state of profound depression. After a lifetime of conservation work motivated by a deep love of the natural world, that journey sapped most of what remained of the determined optimism that had always kept me going. My clean windshield was the *coup de grâce*.

My trip across that prairie landscape was in early August, the peak of nature's fecundity and abundance. Even two decades ago, I would have had to scrub the caked and smeared remains of thousands of insects from my windshield at every fill-up stop. But when I arrived, after 1210 km of driving, I hadn't cleaned my windshield once.

There were no bugs.

My great-great-uncle might have welcomed freedom

from insects. But for me it awakened a deep and hopeless fear. How can nature survive without insects? How can we?

Insects pollinate wildflowers and forbs. They feed baby birds, shrews and bats. They recycle nutrients from animal waste, suppress weeds, keep ungulates from overgrazing, and sustain much of the biodiversity of prairie ecosystems. You can't have nature without insects. You can't have much of anything.

But the landscape I crossed last year was marked with signs of torture. The native prairie was mostly gone, turned upside down and plowed repeatedly until its organic carbon was exhausted and its fertility now only sustained by regular doses of chemical fertilizer. Where once more than 100 species of plants and thousands of species of insects lived in a dense, interconnected, humming web of life, now there were patchwork monocultures of barley, wheat, potatoes, corn, peas, sugar beets and canola. Many of those crops were planted with seeds coated with insect-killing poisons. Others had been genetically modified so that their very pollen is now toxic. Many of the fields were an ugly grey, killed by glyphosate – a carcinogenic plant poison sprayed on crops about to ripen. It speeds up harvest but contaminates our food – and environment.

The family farms that once dotted the landscape were mostly gone. Instead, I saw massive processing plants that turn potatoes into fries and chips, beets into sugar and corn into syrup. The "culture" part of agriculture is vanishing from southern Alberta's irrigation country. Now we talk about agro-industry, as if prairie is meant to be little more than an open-air factory. Many of us fight to save what remains of prairie nature from cultivation and urbanization. But if even the insects are vanishing, what's the point?

On further thought, I don't think my great-great-uncle actually would be happy with this sick version of progress. As a thoughtful observer, surely he would see the deadness – no pipits, curlews or upland sandpipers; no bison; no wildflowers amid prairie grasses. He would see the deadness of the abandoned farms where families once lived good lives. He would sense the spiritual deadness in fields of degraded soil farmed so desperately hard that even the fences have been removed so that crop rows can extend to the very shoulders of gravel grid roads before their yields are trucked to conveyor belt factories.

As a man of God, he would have seen scant evidence of God's creation, or of people who care about it. Neither did I.

COWBOY WELFARE?

Imagine that you and your extended family own a large tract of land full of native vegetation and wildlife. Some of your family fish there in summer or hunt there in the fall. Others simply enjoy the birds, flowers and fresh air. The native prairie on the land would benefit from some grazing, so your family offers a seasonal cattle-grazing lease to a local rancher.

Then one day, much to your surprise, you find some new roads and natural gas wells on the place. The rancher who leases your grass has granted an oil company access to your land in exchange for annual payments – to himself. Not only that, he's put up "No Trespassing" signs around the property and he stops you at the fenceline. "I lease this land," he says. "You can't go in there."

"But it's my land!" you exclaim.

The rancher grins slyly. "Hmmm…" he says. "How much you willing to pay?"

Impossible? Not in Alberta. Our public land is treated

like private property when the government leases out the right to graze our grass. About 5,700 private individuals and groups lease more than 202,000 km² of Alberta Crown land for livestock pasture. They pay less than $3 per Animal Unit Month (or AUM; the equivalent of what a cow and calf eat each month). This is far below market rates for private grazing leases. For example, when my wife and I lease out our private land for grazing, we get about $25 per AUM – eight times more than the government land just across the fence. Red Deer lawyer Bob Scammell, who spent decades fighting for the public's right to enjoy its own land until his death in 2016, called the grazing lease issue "cowboy welfare."

Grazing leases are just that: leases for cows to eat grass. The land still belongs to you and me. But previous Alberta governments allowed lessees to sell their public land leases, rather than surrendering them when they no longer needed the grass themselves. Buying a public grazing lease creates the illusion of land ownership, but that's all it is: an illusion. That land is owned, on our behalf, by our government.

Because of that illusion, grazing lessees have asserted rights not granted by the actual leases. The government even allows leaseholders to act as "gatekeepers" for public access. The presence of livestock is considered reason enough to deny access. Some unscrupulous operators exploit that angle to turn public land into private hunting reserves. After pulling their cattle out for the season, they turn a few horses loose and use the presence of those horses as a reason to deny public hunting access – while giving their friends and family exclusive hunting rights. Some have even been caught illegally charging access fees to guide companies, profiteering not only from our public land but our public wildlife too.

If there's oil and gas under the land, grazing leaseholders can pocket serious profits. Government looks the other way when energy companies pay leaseholders for permission to build roads, pipelines and well pads – even though that money should go to the owner, not the renter. Auditor General Merwan Saher's 2015 annual report estimated that Alberta forgoes more than $25 million annually by way of this unearned subsidy to a wealthy few. Meanwhile, the provincial treasury is bare.

It's not a pretty picture. In fairness, however, neither is it the whole picture. The exploiters are almost certainly a small minority. Most grazing-lease holders are good folks who protect the land from motorized abuse while still welcoming hikers, hunters and others who travel on foot.

Their low grazing fees are more than offset by many volunteer hours of land stewardship. Those good lessees are as offended by the abuses of the few as the rest of us ought to be.

Previous attempts to reform lease policy foundered, largely because Conservative governments depended on politically influential rural elites. A new, less beholden government might do better. Their challenge will be to not throw out the baby with the bathwater. Cattle grazing is, after all, the best economic use of our public rangelands, and grazing is vitally important in sustaining native prairie.

There's no question that non-grazing revenues from public land should flow into government revenues rather than lessees' pockets. Public foot access should be allowed at all times. And grazing-lease fees should reflect private market rates to ensure the fairest return to we the public, who own the resource.

Still – the best grazing lessees work hard to keep our native prairie in prime condition, protect endangered species, remove invasive weeds and sustain wetlands and water supplies. It's only fair that their excellent stewardship should earn discounted grazing rates. Responsible reform should lead to the best lessees paying the same low rents as before – not as cowboy welfare but as fair compensation for their caring stewardship of Alberta's family treasures.

DANGER SPRAY

Glyphosate, better known by its trade name, Roundup, is a popular herbicide. It kills almost anything green, and it's safe too.

Well, maybe not so safe. Recently, courts have begun awarding damages to people whose cancer was deemed to be caused by glyphosate. Studies originally showing glyphosate to be safe had been conducted or paid for by the industry itself. Regulatory agencies – whose job is to protect the public interest from irresponsible decisions by industry – relied on those studies to approve the product. Independent research has belatedly linked the chemical to cancer risk, but regulators and public awareness have yet to catch up.

The sensible thing would be simply not to use Roundup in our gardens anymore. Herbicides are designed to kill living things, after all – it would be a bit naive to assume that they don't affect us. But boycotting Roundup and other related products at the consumer level isn't enough to keep us safe. Governments have approved it for other uses in ways that affect us too.

A common sight along prairie roads nowadays is fields that have turned dirty grey. They look dead. They are. Those fields were sprayed with glyphosate to "cure" crops and prepare them for harvest. You heard that right: some farmers now spray a cancer-causing chemical on crops right before they truck the harvest off to the factories that turn it into food for our kids to eat.

Once-healthy prairie fields become biological deserts while our families absorb chemicals from the food grown there. And chemical company shareholders pocket the profits.

It would probably be wise to avoid foods produced from glyphosate-killed fields. But those foods include corn, soybeans, canola, sugar beets and the alfalfa fed to beef cattle. So-called Roundup-ready varieties of all those crops are now widely used. The chemical companies profit twice: once when they sell farmers the genetically engineered seeds for those crops, and again when they sell the herbicide. Consumers get all the risks and harm. That's a clever business strategy.

Still, assuming we stop using Roundup in our gardens and feed our kids only organic food, we should be okay, right?

Wrong. Because glyphosate gets sprayed all over our public lands too. Forest companies use it to kill aspens, willows, roses, grasses, blueberries – pretty much any plant that won't produce 2×4s and profits.

Most of us live downstream from those poisoned forests. Fortunately, glyphosate binds quickly to soil, so it probably doesn't run off into our drinking water. Well – we can't really be sure of that, since the assurance is based on industry-funded research. One thing's certain: glyphosate turns once-diverse forests into sterilized tree farms. And by turning vegetation into tinder-dry fuel, it also increases forest fire risk.

Forest companies employ public relations staff to persuade us they're managing our public forests responsibly. They assert that logging increases biodiversity by creating more diverse-aged forests, and that replacing crowded old forests with young trees reduces the fire hazard. It sounds good, but it isn't true – especially where those companies spray glyphosate.

When a natural disturbance like fire goes through a forest, a diverse array of pioneer plants appear within months. Aspen, alder and willows stabilize the soil and start to rebuild its organic matter. Legumes transfer nitrogen into the soil, fertilizing it. With no competition for sunlight or rainwater, grasses, strawberries, raspberries, blueberries and roses spread quickly. Wildlife move in to take advantage of all the lush new forage. Fungi and ants colonize the dead tree trunks and become a rich food source for voles, chipmunks, bears and woodpeckers.

But logging is different. Trucks haul away the tree trunks, leaving sparse woody debris for wildlife. Companies plant monocultures of pine or spruce to replace the diverse tree mix they cut down. Some then spray glyphosate to kill everything else. In recent years over 30,000 hectares of Alberta forest have been sprayed annually – almost half of the total area logged.

In central BC the province has been scapegoating wolves after moose numbers dropped by 80 per cent. Logging companies have been killing willow and aspens with glyphosate there for years. That's moose food. Little wonder moose are vanishing. But the companies employ voters, so killing wolves is more politically rewarding than banning a chemical spray.

Glyphosate is not safe; it's disastrous both for human health and for our prairies and forests. But simply being better consumers won't protect us – the herbicide is too widely used in agriculture and forestry. Keeping our families and home places safe will require some active citizenship: we need to demand that our elected governments start putting the public interest ahead of the profits of multinational chemical, agricultural and forestry companies.

AN ENVIRONMENTALIST'S CASE FOR BEEF

"If you knew how meat was made, you'd probably lose your lunch. I know; I'm from cattle country. That's why I became a vegetarian. Meat stinks, and not just for animals but for human health and the environment."

That was Alberta singer-songwriter k.d. lang, in a 1990 television spot for People for the Ethical Treatment of Animals. She grew up in Consort, a small farming town in the Special Areas of Alberta. Until lang bit the hand that fed her, her unique brand of cowboy punk had enjoyed a loyal following in Alberta ranch country. That ended abruptly.

Lang moved away from Alberta and onto greater accomplishments. Although she later expressed some regret for that anti-beef campaign, her sentiment lives on, and not just among the vegetarian fringe. In fact, vegetarians are no longer the fringe. Anti-meat has gone mainstream.

Even *Wall Street International* magazine now offers

reasons for people to shift to vegetable-based substitutes. "The best thing that most people can do for their own health and humanity is don't eat meat," author Rob Smith asserts in a recent article. He argues meat not only clogs our arteries but spreads antibiotic-resistant bacteria. "More importantly," he adds, "mass-produced meat damages the environment and contributes more to global climate change than any other factor."

Cows burp and fart methane, a more potent greenhouse gas than carbon dioxide. Feedlots and other concentrated production systems produce more cows than natural land could support. Too many cows; too much methane. Industrial meat production also puts out lots of CO_2 because it involves trucking heavy animals to feedlots, heating giant barns and applying fertilizers, water and other inputs to the fields that grow animal feeds.

But human health and the climate crisis are not the only reasons why so many people – as many as one-quarter of British women under the age of 25 – are quitting meat. Most supermarket meat comes from factory farms and feedlots where overfed, overmedicated animals die ugly deaths. Bargain prices almost always are a product of animal suffering.

Still, Canadians consume, on average, more than 100 kg

of meat every year. It can be hard to abandon the texture and taste of meat. That's why a growing market for highly realistic vegetable-based counterfeits now makes it possible to give up meat while pretending you didn't.

If you believe conventional rhetoric, our health, environment and very souls all demand that we give up meat. But like many popular truisms, it's not true. In fact, grass-finished beef from range-raised cattle is a far better choice – ethically, environmentally and health-wise – than either feedlot beef or the vegetarian alternatives.

Southern Alberta was bison country before European immigrants showed up and started turning wilderness into farms. Today, grid roads criss-cross plains checkered with fields of grain, canola, peas, corn and other row crops. Domestic cattle crowd sprawling feedlots whose fetid odour sours the prairie wind. And change continues; the family farms that used to line those grid roads have been increasingly replaced by sprawling corporate farms pouring potatoes, pulses, oilseeds and grain into massive factories to be processed into commercial food products.

In the past century and a half, especially in regions served by irrigation infrastructure, the land has gone from ecologically diverse prairie, to small mixed farms, to agro-industry monocultures. At each step we've lost natural diversity and human community. Most native prairie wildlife is now classified as at risk.

On a still summer afternoon it can seem like even the ghosts have abandoned irrigation country. Genetically modified crops grow on deadened soils kept productive only by constant addition of chemical fertilizers, frequent applications of pesticides that kill weeds and bugs, and water pumped from dying rivers. Alberta's whole system of food production increasingly runs on oil, electricity, chemicals and ecocide.

It's not a pretty picture. But if you believe that only plant-based diets can save us, it's a picture of the future. Big business, environmentalists and animal rights advocates rarely find common ground, but they seem united by the idea that we should eat lower down the food chain.

It's worth noting, however, that the most fervent fake-meat boosterism comes from multinational agribusiness companies that profit by forcing land to mass-produce those commodities – nature be damned. Their con job could end up costing us not only what remains of Alberta's native prairies but also one of our best bets for storing carbon safely away in the soil.

Peas are the magic ingredient in phony meat. Agri-food corporations combine peas with other vegetable products to create convincing facsimiles of not only meat but also fish, eggs and dairy. Fake foods are no fad; investors are excited. According to a recent Bloomberg business report, shares of Beyond Meat – which markets plant-based meat substitutes to fast-food chains and supermarkets – tripled in value on the company's first day of public trading. Global pea production is projected to increase fourfold by 2025, with Canada making up 30 per cent of that growth. Almost half of that will be in Alberta. Cargill – a global agro-industry conglomerate – is among companies ramping up pea production in expectation that consumers will abandon real meat once they taste the facsimiles. Ironically, Cargill is also one of Alberta's biggest meat processors; either way they win.

Peas and other plants used for fake meat are grown as monocultures on cultivated soil. That soil, originally built by living prairie, now contains far less organic carbon. Trucks bring synthetic fertilizers from distant factories and then farmers use machinery to apply them to the depleted soils. In the drier parts of the province farmers also pump massive amounts of water out of prairie rivers to irrigate the fields. The native fish and floodplain forests of the lower Bow and Oldman rivers are now as endangered as the wildlife that used to live where those crops now grow. Irrigation runoff restores some water to the rivers, but it arrives full of fertilizer, herbicide and insecticide residues.

Vegetable-based non-meat appeals to consumers who care about their environmental impact. Ironic, then, that those manufactured foods are, in fact, the product of ecological violence – zombie soils kept productive by massive amounts of petroleum, chemicals and water.

There is an alternative: real beef. Like bison, domestic cattle produce meat by grazing plants we can't digest and converting them to protein. No ecological violence required. In fact, most native prairie grasses actually need animals such as bison or cattle to graze them. By cropping growing grasses, responsibly managed cattle herds constantly stimulate plants to grow new material both above and below ground. That sustains both native biodiversity and living soils. Living soils store carbon and water. In a world facing catastrophic climate disruption, that's important.

Rachel Herbert was a vegetarian for 18 years – ironic, given that her great-grandfather founded Alberta's historic OH Ranch back in 1882. Rachel's mom inherited some of the family land in the Porcupine Hills around the same time as Rachel fell in love with a cowboy and they decided to make a life together in agriculture. The growing season in the Porcupines is too short for row crops, so livestock were the only option. But the Herberts quickly decided they couldn't be part of a system that forces weaned calves into feedlots.

"I was a vegetarian not for health reasons but because I love animals," Rachel Herbert says, "so I thought: if you love animals, you can't eat them. But … we need to nourish ourselves and look after the land, and what way can we do that that fits with this environment? Raising beef on pasture is actually an amazing way to feed our family and … a lot of other families."

Rachel and Tyler Herbert now operate Trail's End Beef. The ranch's top priorities are livestock welfare and range health. They finish their cattle on grass, not on grain, and slaughter them on their home pastures rather than in a crowded meat factory. They sell the meat directly to consumers, many of whom bring their kids when they drive out to Nanton to pick up beef orders. Helping urban consumers connect with family-based agriculture has proven to be one of the most rewarding aspects of their business model. Rachel Herbert sees each customer as a partner.

"We try to express to them that just as the land is important and the water is important, that their role as a consumer is another part of that full circle that keeps the ranch going around from year to year. They're integral … they're part of the ecosystem."

As a former vegetarian, Rachel respects those who choose that lifestyle for ethical reasons. "Personally, I'm still vegetarian unless I'm eating meat that I know the source of," she says. "It makes you so much more conscious of the meat you do eat if you're considering the family and the land that raised it for you."

"Consumers are right to have valid concerns about our industrial agriculture and food system," she adds, "but I don't think Beyond Meat is the answer; it's really just another piece of the same problem."

Alberta farmers annually harvest crops from an estimated 25 million acres (9.3 million hectares) of cultivated land. The soil that produces those crops was originally rich in organic carbon stored in the roots of native plants. Native prairie can contain as many as 100 different plant species, all rooted at different depths. Some roots reach almost four metres deep. As those roots die back each winter and are replaced in spring, they fill the soil with organic carbon. Cultivation kills the native vegetation, leaving that organic material to decompose. The carbon escapes back into the atmosphere as carbon dioxide.

Soil researcher Eric Bremer did a peer-reviewed study in 2008 to see if livestock production – by stimulating plant growth – could help return that carbon to the soil. He estimated that, depending on the ecological region, decades' worth of cultivation released between 22 and 40 metric tons of carbon per hectare into the atmosphere. In theory, based on his numbers, restoring most of Alberta's farmland to prairie could sequester well more than 250 million metric tons of carbon.

That won't happen. Farming is economically important. Crop agriculture is here to stay.

Even so, many thousands of hectares of shallow soils or dry land ought never to have been broken, and now produce only marginal returns for farmers. Turning them back to cattle production could be part of a wise climate strategy. It would also restore wildlife habitat.

"I live in the Special Areas," says Colleen Biggs. The Special Areas lie north of the Red Deer River where early settlers tried to crop the land but failed during the Dirty Thirties. Land repossessed for unpaid taxes reverted to wild prairie. As a result, many of Alberta's endangered prairie wildlife species still thrive there. "We've only got half an inch of topsoil on most of the ranch," says Biggs. "It's not arable land. That's why beef is important. There are so many marginal soils, especially on the Great Plains, that should never have been farmed.

"Think about the petrochemical inputs and water that are required to farm in soil that isn't arable – basically, it's an artificial environment, it's devoid of life…. If you can convert that land back to livestock production, those costs are gone and the soil can start storing carbon again and we could get back some of the biodiversity we've lost."

Colleen and Dylan Biggs own the TK Ranch ("Ethical By Nature") near k.d. lang's childhood home. Their rural community is united in defence of agriculture, but not everyone agrees on everything. One point of contention: water. The lack of reliable water is one reason that the Special Areas were so designated in the first place. In fact, four years into the latest drought, the TK Ranch is struggling financially because of the scarcity of local hay for winter feed.

Municipal governments and community boosters want to pipe water from the Red Deer River to area communities and farms. Besides providing better domestic water, the proposed Special Areas Water Supply Project would irrigate an additional 3,240 acres (1311 hectares). But cultivating that land would release more carbon into the atmosphere and destroy critical wildlife habitat. Use of chemicals and fossil fuels would increase too – in fact, most of the project's ongoing costs would be for energy to power water pumps.

Diverting river water might make life better for the area's scattered farm and ranch families, but it would further impair two of the world's most threatened habitats: native prairie and riparian (river-bottom) ecosystems.

That's why Colleen Biggs opposes the proposed water project. She was an ecologist with the Alberta Wilderness Association when she met Dylan, a young rancher who had embraced holistic range management. Today, the health of the native prairie and nearby watercourses matters as much to them as the well-being of their animals.

They encountered the dark side of industrial farming when they established a sales outlet in irrigation country closer to Calgary.

"I love the ranch and I'm so committed to protecting that ecosystem," she says. "I built our little farm store [east of Calgary] five years ago and it was just devoid of life.... I remember sitting on the front deck here and thinking: 'This is just so quiet. It's really terrible.' And people around here, they don't know what it's supposed to sound like. The cacophony of sound [birds, frogs, insects] back at the ranch – literally, I have to get up and close my window at night."

The same intensive agriculture that silenced so much of the natural music near TK Ranch's farm store could soon bring that same stillness closer to their home ranch, if irrigation proponents get their way.

And it's not just the Special Areas whose native grassland and prairie rivers are threatened by proposals for irrigation expansion. Farther south, farmers want a new irrigation dam on the Milk River. Existing irrigation districts east of Calgary and Lethbridge, having found ways to use less water, don't want to return the extra to overexploited prairie rivers; they're looking for new land to irrigate too.

Now peas are in demand for fake meat. That makes the prospect of more irrigated cropland even more appealing to some. Little wonder many Alberta ranchers and prairie conservation advocates are worried.

Profit margins for beef production are lower than for most row crops. Grass-finished beef is even more challenging. Whereas a traditional rancher can ship 18-month-old animals to a feedlot to be fattened on grain and then slaughtered, it can take as long as 26–29 months to finish cattle on grass. The cost of feeding and caring for them through two winters means ranchers like the Herberts and Biggs have to charge higher prices for meat. Unfortunately, some consumers don't care if their meat is from miserable, overmedicated feedlot calves whose feed comes from biological deserts – just so long as it's cheap.

Still, many consumers want to eat responsibly. The same considerations that can make principled shoppers vulnerable to the green-wash claims of purveyors of fake meat can also lead them to buy ethically raised meat from the Trail's End Beefs and TK Ranches of the world. Market forces may seem poised to replace what remains of our native prairies with chemical-saturated pea fields bleeding carbon dioxide into the atmosphere, but there's also a social cross-current flowing back to beef and wild prairie.

Rachel Herbert suggests marginal farmland should be restored as cattle range. "Perennial grasslands are one of our best carbon sinks," she points out, "and in terms of wildlife habitat, regeneration and soil health, there are just so many advantages. We hear about people who want to save the Amazon, when we have this disappearing grassland ecosystem in our own backyard. We're never going to get those native grasslands back – but any type of perennial grassland system would be better."

Respected Alberta botanist and environmentalist Cheryl Bradley agrees, but she says wild prairie, once gone, is almost impossible to restore. Bradley credits ranchers for helping the province hang onto what little remains of our native prairie biodiversity. "Some ecosystems simply aren't very appropriate to grow vegetarian food because the inputs are so high for whatever outputs you get. The foothills, for example, aren't suitable for cultivation, so they're not going to feed vegetarians. Raising livestock … is the highest and best use of this land."

Irrigation expansion schemes that replace responsibly raised beef with crops used for plant-based ersatz meat leave Bradley cold. "It's completely inappropriate to say all meat production is bad. Because it is happening on landscapes that can sustain it, if managed well, and we've got all the biodiversity besides, and the carbon storage ... a whole lot of values come from this land."

With regard to restoring cultivated fields to prairie, though, Bradley says the moister grassland types may be lost for good. "I think it's feasible in some areas, but it depends a lot on the ecology of the area. So the dry, mixed grassland can be restored, it seems, and I think that's mainly because fewer invasive, non-native species thrive in those arid low-carbon soils. But when you get to the mixed grass prairies farther west and the fescue prairie, our experience is that we don't have much success in restoring them."

Few consumers want to be complicit in the destruction of endangered native prairie and river ecosystems. Most would likely prefer agriculture that stores carbon in living soil rather than pouring it into the atmosphere. But animal welfare is also critical to many debating the merits of meat. And while many Alberta ranchers do an exemplary job of protecting prairie biodiversity and soils, most still send their calves to feedlots to end their lives bloated with grain, knee-deep in manure. Those feedlots rely on cultivated crops no less than fake-meat burgers do.

And our health matters too, after all. The white fat that marbles feedlot-finished beef is as dangerous for humans as hydrogenated oils.

All of which leads back to ranchers like the Biggs and the Herberts who offer a third choice: grass-raised, grass-finished and ethically cared-for beef. Like other ranchers, their business model protects grasslands and stores carbon safely underground. But by finishing their animals on grass they also keep those animals out of unhealthy, stressful environments. And the yellow fat in grass-finished beef is healthy for humans.

The Audubon Society's Conservation Ranching Program promotes us ranches that meet the same high standards as Alberta's grass-finished cattle operations. More than 40 retail stores and 11 online sales outlets now sell meat carrying the Audubon label, reassuring buyers that their meat helps sustain nature. But it's only for American ranches. Colleen Biggs hopes to develop a similar program in Canada, for Canadians.

In the meantime, we all need protein in our diets. That means we have choices to make. Choices come with consequences.

We can keep buying meat from animals raised or finished under inhumane conditions and fed grains or other feeds they were never meant to consume. At the very least, we can comfort ourselves that buying Alberta beef at the supermarket helps ranchers sustain the wild prairie habitats where their livestock graze – before being shipped to the feedlot.

Or we can shift to engineered meat substitutes produced at the cost of sickened soils, more carbon emissions and lost biodiversity – marketed to well-intentioned consumers by green-washed multinationals who could care less about native grasslands, prairie rivers, endangered wildlife or the growing climate crisis.

Either choice makes us partners in the mass commodification of food and the continuing degradation of Alberta ecosystems and soils for row-crop farming.

Or we can put true conservation on our tables by buying grass-finished beef and free-range pork and chickens from the growing number of Albertan ranch families working to produce ethical meat. That choice costs consumers more. But it costs the land, and the future, far less. And by bringing consumers and ranchers together as partners in a food production model that keeps wild prairies intact, treats animals with respect and improves the ability of soils to store both carbon and water, its ultimate value might be priceless.

5

PARKS

MANDATE CREEP

National Parks were never for tourists.

I retired from a career with Parks Canada a few years ago, not long after signing off on a management plan that prescribed a 2 per cent annual increase in visitor numbers.

Local businesses were ecstatic that the new plan seemed finally to acknowledge tourism growth as a priority. They loved the prospect of overheated credit card machines. Environmental groups who have long fought over-development in our national parks were outraged.

The debate was moot: Parks Canada didn't even have to try to meet the growth target. Tourism in Banff National Park alone grew by more than 30 per cent between 2010 and 2017.

As if that massive increase didn't strain already-over-crowded parks enough, the federal government made entry to all Canada's national parks free in 2017. Banff and Jasper – with their gate revenues erased – had to establish new temporary parking lots, rent buses to move people around, hire extra staff to direct traffic and cope with a spike in wildlife conflicts caused by naive new visitors.

A lot of Canadians simply avoided the mess.

People like simple ideas and sharp contrasts. That's why, for most of their 134-year history, media coverage has framed the core conundrum facing our national parks as "balance." It's easier to think in binary terms about a simple conflict between use and protection than to dig deeper into why traffic jams, rather than the peaceful enjoyment of nature, increasingly define the park experience.

I had coffee with a former colleague the other day. She told me that the discussion in the mountain national parks now is not how to grow tourism but how to cope with massive overcrowding. They are even asking the Walt Disney Company for ideas.

Here's an idea: do only what you're mandated to do.

The Canada National Parks Act establishes the core mandate for our national parks. The dedication clause in that law has remained unchanged since 1930, in spite of numerous other changes to the law that gives our parks their existence. That's no accident; it defines what Canadians want their parks to be.

"The national parks of Canada are hereby dedicated to the people of Canada for their benefit, education and enjoyment … and the parks shall be maintained and made use of so as to leave them unimpaired for the enjoyment of future generations."

That clause makes no reference to tourism. In fact, the word "tourism" appears nowhere in the parks act. Our national parks are dedicated only to Canadians – not to visitors from the US, Germany, Japan, Korea or Great Britain.

But, from the very beginning, Canada has flogged its parks to the world as tourism destinations. Politicians and parkocrats alike boast about their role in helping Canada's balance of trade. Mass tourism may frivolously generate millions of tons of greenhouse gases and create traffic grid-lock in once-peaceful parks, but that's okay because each tourist leaves a whack of foreign dollars behind – new dollars, compared to the recycled ones we Canadians spend.

The powerful influence tourism operators wield offers more evidence of how bad this mandate creep has become. When Rocky Mountains Park (now Banff National Park) was first established, the government recognized that the private sector was better than government at providing basic services – lodgings, food, recreational gear – to the Canadians who were expected to resort to their new park. So, although national parks were meant to remain in the public domain, government made carefully limited provision for businesses to lease property and sell services that visitors would need. It was a pragmatic compromise meant to support – not supplant – the park's core mandate.

Banff today has tattoo parlours, marijuana shops, high-end fashion outlets, bulk mail contractors and jewelry stores – hardly the kinds of essential services Canadians need in order to benefit, be educated about and enjoy our natural heritage.

Passage of the 1998 Parks Canada Agency Act helped lock in the shift from inviting Canadians to experience nature to making money off of tourism. Meant to buffer Parks Canada from political interference, the new law also made the agency reliant on visitor fees. In effect, it codified a new, unofficial mandate: processing credit cards. Instead of riding the brake pedal on profit-hungry businesses, Parks Canada became one.

Parks Canada is today almost entirely captive to the tourism industry. Environmental groups warn against turning our national parks into versions of Disneyland. Ironic, then, that park bureaucrats are now consulting with Disney for advice on how to cope with mobs of foreign tourists.

The solution to this mess is not better tourism

management; Canada's national parks were never meant for tourists. If there even is a solution, it has to start with acknowledging that our national parks have no legal mandate for international tourism. They exist solely to help Canadians better know, love and protect our nation's natural heritage.

STORM OVER THE CASTLE

It should have been easy, but it wasn't.

It should have been easy because the headwaters of the Castle, Carbondale and Waterton rivers were always meant to be a park. Until 1928, the windy mountain valleys southwest of Pincher Creek actually were a park: part of Waterton Lakes National Park. That year the federal and provincial governments agreed to shrink the boundaries of Waterton to include just the scenery around the Waterton Lakes and the streams draining to them. Everything else became provincial land.

But the Castle was meant to be a park. The region is the most biologically diverse in Alberta. Its mountain landscape – including some of the planet's oldest sedimentary rock – is spectacular. Wildlife – from mountain goats and bighorn sheep to wolverines and grizzlies – abounds. Threatened species of trout thrive in some of the prettiest streams in the world.

Unprotected, it was soon under threat. Shell Canada

found natural gas under the Castle in the late 1950s and began building roads and drilling wells. Locals who had kept their backyard paradise secret for years grew alarmed at the pace of industrial development. So in 1968 the Pincher Creek Fish and Game Association and others petitioned the Alberta government to restore the Castle's protection.

Six years later the province's Department of Recreation, Parks and Wildlife recommended that the Castle be granted provincial park status. But Alberta had a petro-government; that wasn't going to happen. The government decided to develop Kananaskis Country instead.

Gas well roads and pipelines opened the once-pristine Castle wilds to the next and, arguably, greater threat: off-highway vehicles. OHVs were rare when I first ventured into the high country in the 1970s, but as technology improved and oil and gas wealth made the machines affordable, more and more Albertans began to use them for access and play. Mud holes and eroding gullies metastasized through the Castle. OHV-crossed streams became choked with sediment. Landscape abuse became the new normal not just there but on public land across Alberta.

A government-mandated 1992 Castle Access Management Plan restricted off-roaders to a few designated routes. They ignored it. Nobody enforced it. Things got worse.

A group of local ranchers, outfitters, outdoors people and tourism operators – the Castle-Crown Wilderness Coalition – laboured for decades to persuade the government that the Castle's landscape was too precious to be sold out, carved up and vandalized by noisy motor vehicles. But after the release of its 1992 weak-soup access plan, the government's only tangible action was to invite Spray Lakes Sawmills to clear-cut the area's timber. It was just the way Alberta had become.

The NDP went into Alberta's 2015 election expecting to lose. Maybe that's why their platform was so ambitious. Among their promises: to protect the Castle area as a park again. After their surprise win, Shannon Phillips, a fiercely intelligent NDP veteran, was appointed Minister of Environment and Parks.

Her department promptly announced plans to restore protection to the Castle. Its first step, in September 2015, was to shut down logging. In February 2017 the government announced final boundaries for a provincial park and a wildland park in the Castle. The draft park management plan released at the same time called for all OHV use to be phased out.

Enraged off-roaders responded with protest rallies, letters to the editor, hate mail to the minister and premier.

"The thing is," said noted biologist Lorne Fitch, who has spent much of his career dealing with the landscape and stream damage caused by off-roading, "these guys never had anyone say no to them before. And it was an NDP minister, a woman, saying no."

In 2015 Phillips had said OHV use would continue in the parks. That was before she consulted a broad panel of science experts and before Albertans, very few of whom use OHVs for recreation, responded to the government's request for public comments. It quickly became clear that for the Castle parks to be truly protected world-class parks, off-roading had to go. For finally making the right choice, Phillips endured weeks of insults and threats by a furious minority who thought bully tactics would force her to back down. They were wrong.

"The public doesn't really like change," Phillips told me, quoting former Saskatchewan Premier Allan Blakeney. "They like the outcome of change, but they don't like change."

The outcome of this change is that, almost a century later, Albertans have won park status back for the spectacular Castle area. Even better: the brief, ugly era of OHV overuse in our headwaters may finally be ending.[3]

HUNTING IN JASPER

A few years ago Sykes Powderface and I visited a mouldering old cabin in Banff National Park. He told me that a Chinese immigrant market gardener who once lived there used to trade vegetables to Sykes's father in exchange for bighorn sheep meat. Some of that meat likely came from national park sheep. Sykes is a Stoney Nakoda Elder and his people have traditionally used the high valleys and passes that, starting with the 1885 establishment of Rocky Mountains Park, became Canada's first national park. The park was never the Stoneys' idea.

For many Canadians, national parks are remnants of pristine wilderness, meant to be protected from people. That idea is founded in fallacy. No Canadian landscape was unmarked by human presence when European settlers first decided to give themselves some parks. What looked to the colonizers like untouched wilderness was in fact a mosaic of cultural landscapes shaped by Indigenous use of fire, plant culture, hunting and other practices. Those wilds were home places.

Indigenous Canadians, however, were soon unwelcome in many of our older, better-known parks. In the case of Banff, in fact, the park superintendent insisted they be banished. In his 1903 annual report, Howard Douglas described the Stoneys as ruthless hunters whose depredations were wiping out game herds.

Conveniently ignoring hunting and poaching by growing hordes of white settlers, Douglas persuaded Ottawa to expand the park to over 4,000 square miles – much larger than today. The story Sykes told me, and the one by which his people came to know Banff, was that the Mounties set up a guard station at the new park gate to keep Indians out. Tourists were welcome in places where the Stoneys had always camped, gathered medicines, collected pipestone, hunted and prayed; only the original inhabitants weren't.

Eventually, the Stoney people were allowed to visit their homelands again, but only as visitors. It wasn't until 2010 that a different superintendent formally welcomed them home. A small step toward reconciliation, it was a very long time coming.

Last fall Jasper National Park took a much bigger step, one that soon became controversial with those who would rather that reconciliation take place outside the national parks and not involve any real change to the status quo.

The ancestors of the Simpcw people lived along the Athabasca River valley. Fur traders called them the Snaring Indians, from the traps they set for large animals. Jasper's Snaring River got its name from these people. But in the 19th century, decimated both by smallpox and armed conflict with newcomers, the Simpcw retreated west to the Fraser River valley. In the early 20th century, the government forcibly relocated them to a reserve near Kamloops.

The Simpcw are among several Indigenous groups collaborating with Parks Canada to reconcile Jasper's history of expropriation and exclusion with our constitutional obligation to respect this country's original people. In October 2017, the Simpcws held their first traditional community hunt on their ancestral lands in well over a century. Nine hunters and several support members camped near the Snaring River. They killed three elk, two bighorn sheep and a deer. The meat and hides were shared in the community, just as it had long been done.

Chief Nathan Matthew said, "Acting freely in our own traditional territory, representing ourselves as a Nation and having our people exercise our rights through this harvest, means the world to us. [It] gives us a better memory of Jasper National Park and helps deal with some of the intergenerational trauma of being forced from the land. Together, we are working in a true spirit of reconciliation with Parks Canada to move forward together through mutual respect."

Those who were surprised by the idea of a traditional community hunt in a national park probably shouldn't have been. Land claim agreements in Canada's north have created modern national parks around a co-management model that always includes ongoing hunting and gathering by Indigenous Peoples. Local Cree communities have long hunted and trapped in Wood Buffalo National Park.

Even Banff has dipped its toes into these once unheard-of waters. The park has culled up to 20 elk from the Banff townsite area each winter since 2006, to keep the animals from congregating in town. Hunters from the Siksika and Stoney Nakoda First Nations join parks staff, help select the animals to be killed and take about a third of the culled animals back to their communities. It's not hunting the way Sykes's father did it, but it beats being turned away at the gates.

Jasper has now taken a much bigger step toward turning Canada's national park idea into one that includes the people who lived here first. There are those who worry that last fall's Simpcw community hunt may have estab-lished a precedent.

They're right. It did. It's about time.

BEARS AND BRAINS

Winston Churchill is reputed to have said, "History is written by the victors." In other words: consider the source before believing an assertion. Another example of "he who holds the pen" relates to intelligence. For centuries, the prevailing view was that humans are the only intelligent species. All other creatures rely on instinct and habit. But, of course, when humans assert our monopoly on intelligence, there's a fairly huge conflict of interest involved. Self-interest dictates that intelligence has to look like what our brains do.

How do we recognize intelligence? The *Cambridge English Dictionary* defines it as "the ability to learn, understand and make judgments or have opinions that are based on reason." That's a definition created for humans, by humans. According to us, intelligence is an attribute that only evolved when our predecessors came down out of the trees and starting dodging big carnivores.

Like bears. Bear 64, for example – a grizzly who lived

near the town of Banff for 24 years before disappearing about three years ago. She raised at least two sets of cubs in the most crowded corner of Banff National Park. There's lots of natural food there, but the area is a jumble of roads, a railroad, parking lots, ski resorts and a major town. All her cubs ultimately died unnatural deaths because the lower Bow valley is a tough place to survive. A bear can find many ways to get into trouble.

Or to avoid trouble. Indeed, my first encounter with Bear 64, several years ago, got me seriously questioning whether humans have a monopoly on intelligence.

It was a spring morning at the western entrance to the Town of Banff. As usual, the place was crawling with motorized tourists. Bear 64 emerged from the woods east of the Norquay road, two half-grown cubs in tow, and paused at the edge of the road clearing. She evidently wanted to take her cubs west, across the road, into the rich forage of the Vermilion Lakes wetlands.

As she tested the air and studied the situation, cars began to stop. She glanced at each car briefly, but the stationary vehicles were of little interest. She was more interested in figuring out how to get her cubs safely across the road without colliding with a moving car.

Doors began to open. People with cellphones jostled

to the edge of the asphalt. As the crowd grew, muttered exclamations of excitement grew to a happy babble. Bear 64's cubs, evidently more interested in play and food than in the growing herd of intelligent humans beginning to hem them in, wandered about as if nothing unusual were happening. I could see that their mom was getting a bit stressed as she tried to keep an eye on them and, at the same time, figure out her options in an increasingly chaotic scene.

She looked right, left, back, forward – and finally made up her mind. Carefully avoiding eye contact with any of the excited paparazzi, she gathered her cubs behind her and stepped up onto the pavement. The nearest people snapped hasty pictures and retreated, some running, to stand by their vehicles. Others who had been hastening across the road paused and stared in sudden fear.

Bear 64 ushered her cubs through the last remaining gap among the cars, veered left to avoid some people emerging from behind a camper and walked calmly down into the safety of the forest.

Once again, as she had done pretty much every day of her long life, she had used her learning to understand a situation and make a rational judgment about how to deal with it. Her intelligence had kept her and her cubs alive for another day.

Watching the behaviour of the humans, however, I couldn't help but be reminded of a conversation with a Waterton-area rancher. He said that for many years the prevalent view among his neighbours was that there was no point putting cattle up the Front Range canyons because too many would get killed by grizzlies. "When we started putting cow–calf pairs up there instead of yearlings," he said, "the loss rate dropped right off."

Yearling cattle aren't particularly bright when it comes to bears. When seeing something new, they often crowd in for a closer look, almost like they're tempting fate. When surrounded by others, they lose any vestige of intelligence and react instinctively, like a dumb mob.

I'd just watched a crowd of so-called intelligent humans act like yearling cattle, just as they too often do when a bear appears on a roadside. Bear 64 was the only one there who demonstrated intelligence. But she, and all her offspring, are gone today.

Bears are indeed intelligent, but that's not enough. Their survival requires us, too, to be as intelligent as we like to think we are.

DON'T FENCE ME IN

Try and picture them all. On his first visit to the Waterton area in 1865, John ("Kootenai") Brown wrote: "The prairie as far as we could see east, north and west was one living mass of buffalo. Thousands of head there were, far thicker than ever range cattle grazed the bunch grass of the foothills.... None of our party up to this time had ever seen a buffalo."

They were seeing a doomed species. Deliberately and wastefully slaughtered by a newcomer people, within barely two decades North America's great bison herds – once totalling more than 30 million – were all but gone. Only empty grasslands and bleached bones remained.

Annual Métis bison hunts, in Brown's day, sometimes filled more than a thousand Red River carts with bison meat. Those hunts had ended by 1880 for lack of bison. The US army had overseen the killing of millions of the great beasts; desperate Indigenous people and wasteful colonizers had hunted down the scattered survivors. By 1889, barely 1,200 North American plains bison remained.

Although a few hundred wood bison survived in the far north, the continent's largest land mammal was gone from the plains, foothills and mountains of what would become the province of Alberta. Soon even the bleached skulls and bones vanished, gathered up by settlers and sold for fertilizer.

To the Indigenous people of this place, the empty plains and forests were a silent horror. Their cultures, languages, spiritual traditions and livelihood were all, to varying degrees, tied up in those massive beasts. Losing the bison was like having their very souls torn out. But Canada's first prime minister, John A. Macdonald, thought it a very good thing.

"I am not at all sorry," he said to Canada's House of Commons in faraway Ottawa. "So long as there was a hope that bison would come into the country, there was no means of inducing the Indians to settle down on their reserves."

Alberta became a province at a time when wild nature was considered a godless waste awaiting the plows of immigrant farmers to bring it to its God-intended use. Alberta's natural ecosystems were simply raw material for future commerce. The people whose identity resided in the land and its bison were in the way.

With the bison gone, those people retreated to Indian reserves to live as paupers. Bison range got turned upside down and planted to wheat. Much of it was fenced and filled with domestic cattle. When hungry wolves and bears had to shift from wild prey to domestic meat too, the newcomers put out strychnine baits. Ravens and eagles fed at the poison baits and the skies grew emptier. Insects and amphibians that had lived in bison wallows and dung became rare; some, like the Rocky Mountain locust, went extinct. The prairie wind hissed with the hollow lament of ghosts.

Everything had changed.

Now, however, the bison are coming back. Everything may be about to change again.

It could be argued that bison have been back for a while. Starting with a small herd that the Canadian government bought from Montana rancher Michel Pablo and installed between 1907 and 1912 in Elk Island National Park and just south of Wainwright, the number of fenced-in bison in Alberta grew steadily through the 20th century. The

Wainwright Buffalo Park was closed in 1939, but Elk Island has since become the world's most important bison conservation facility. Commercial herds have also grown to feed a growing demand among consumers for high-quality meat. Many of Canada's more than 120,000 captive bison are now raised on Alberta ranches.

But as Lethbridge-area bison rancher Cody Spencer points out, commercial bison contribute little to either ecosystem health or Indigenous cultural renewal; they are simply livestock. Spencer feels there is both room and a real need in Alberta for wild bison too. Alberta's regulatory regime, unfortunately, doesn't allow that. With the exception of two small herds – one in the Hay–Zama Lakes area on the Northwest Territories boundary and another south of Wood Buffalo National Park – bison are conspicuously absent from the province's wildlife regulations and its formal listings of species at risk. In Alberta, unlike other provinces and territories, wild bison can't officially exist.

Colin Kure would like that situation to continue. Kure ranches near Rocky Mountain House and is active in the Alberta Fish and Game Association. He speaks for both the ranching community and many hunters in protesting the recent reintroduction of wild bison to Banff National Park. Parks Canada brought ten bison cows and six bulls to the park's remote Panther River valley in 2016 and put them into a fenced pasture where, the following spring, the cows gave birth to the first calves of what will soon be a free-ranging herd. Parks Canada plans to turn the bison loose in 2018, with strategically placed fences to keep them from heading east into the foothills where Kure and other ranchers pasture their cattle.

Ranchers worry that government fences won't stop those bison. They expect the big animals to become a costly problem: competing with domestic livestock for forage, breaking down ranch fences and spreading disease. Some hunters fear that bison could displace valued big-game animals such as bighorn sheep and elk from long-treasured hunting grounds, including the Ya Ha Tinda grasslands along the upper Red Deer River.

"There isn't a fence in the world that will hold bison if a pack of wolves gets on them. And a fence that's permeable to elk, deer, bighorn sheep and moose certainly will not contain bison.... Those animals will move," Kure wrote in a letter meant to mobilize public opposition to the plan.

Bill Hunt is Banff National Park's resource conservation

manager responsible for the bison restoration initiative. He respects Kure's concerns. His staff spent two years trying to perfect a fencing design that would work in the park's wilderness landscape. Ranchers who raise semi-domesticated bison have found that six-strand barbed-wire fences, especially when buttressed with one or two strands of electric wire, will keep bison confined. It's the other animals that are a problem: those fences stop them too.

The Banff recovery team couldn't come up with a fence that would stop bison but let other animals move freely through their home ranges. Instead, they are counting on a high-tech solution. The eastern escape routes for park bison are fenced with industry-standard fences, but where monitoring has shown that those fences block trails that are important for elk, sheep and other animals, parks staff tie the six strands up into two strips, creating a gap big enough for wildlife to slip through. All the original bison wear radio-collars that send out a warning signal when the bison wander close to those critical fence-crossing locations. When bison are nearby, park biologists unbundle the wire to block the animals until they wander deeper into the park again.

It's a labour-intensive and costly approach, and it will only work as long as the original radio collars work. Parks

Canada isn't collaring calves born in the park, so un-collared bison will soon outnumber the original bunch. And critics still point out a big weakness in the fencing plan: rivers draining out of Banff National Park flood every spring. Fences are bound to wash out. Bison will escape eventually.

Still, Hunt suspects that fears about wide-ranging bison may be overblown. "Historically bison were a nomadic species but I think a lot of that was the sheer number of animals. They would deplete a food resource and move on. So right from the get-go, managing herd size has always been a key concept here."

The Panther River experiment is premised on the idea that bison born in Banff to young cows who had their first calves in Banff will consider those high valleys their home ranges. It's the same approach tried successfully in Grasslands National Park a decade ago. Then, by keeping herd size within the capacity of the mountain grasslands to feed them, park staff hope the bison will have little inclination to wander.

How to keep the herd size down? There really is only one answer: hunting. Although wolves hunt them successfully in places such as Wood Buffalo National Park, bison are hard to kill. Wild carnivores usually prefer smaller prey.

Hunting – either by Indigenous people or licensed sport hunters or both – will have to play a role.

"There are lots of hunters in the Panther Corners area [downstream from the bison reintroduction area] already," says Hunt. "There's access for horse-drawn wagons. We're hoping there wouldn't be any bison shot when the herd is small and every animal is genetically important, but when the herd gets a little larger, hunting would be a fantastic thing. Not only would it help with population goals but it might encourage bison to stay inside the park."

The sticky issue remains: What is the status of a park bison when it wanders across the boundary? "In Alberta," Hunt says, "bison are considered livestock. Because our program is to restore them as wildlife, our bison are not livestock. They're classified as wildlife in Banff. If and when they do leave the park, they would be non-status."

That means they can be shot on sight – something that appears unlikely to change soon. Alberta's Wildlife Act authorizes the minister to change the status of a species of animal only on the recommendation of an advisory committee. But the Endangered Species Conservation Committee has been inactive since before the last election, caught up in the government-wide review of agencies, boards and commissions that has been dragging on since

2015. Wild bison that wander out into the Alberta foothills will remain unprotected and unmanaged until the government gets around to classifying them as wildlife.

While those worried about wild bison are focused on Banff's new herd, they should also look farther south, where wild plains bison – unmanaged by parks staff – will soon almost certainly reappear.

In the spring of 2016 a herd of 87 bison went by truck from Elk Island National Park to the Blackfeet Reservation in northern Montana to serve as the nucleus of a new free-ranging conservation herd. The herd, which has already grown to more than 150, ranges a large ranch on the northern edge of the Blackfeet reservation – adjacent to the Alberta border. Although some new fencing went up around the boundaries of the ranch before the new herd's arrival, it's not nearly to the standard of Banff's fences. Blackfeet bison will likely wander freely into southern Alberta within a couple of years.

Ranchers north of the border are worried. As one area rancher confided to me: "It took me a while to understand the spiritual importance of the bison to the Blackfeet, and I do. But I don't know what to expect. Those bison are going to end up nose to nose with Alberta cattle. Are they diseased? Who knows? Nobody has talked to us."

Disease concerns are understandable. When the Pablo–Allard bison arrived in the Wainwright reserve, area cattle herds already harboured tuberculosis and brucellosis. The cattle infected the bison and the diseases spread quickly in the overcrowded reserve. A few years later, in what came to be known as the century's biggest conservation blunder, Canadian bureaucrats decided to close the reserve and ship young animals north to the Peace–Athabasca delta, where the world's last known population of wood bison had recently been found. They rationalized that the young bison might be disease-free. They were wrong. The new immigrants not only contaminated Wood Buffalo National Park's wood bison with plains bison genes, they also spread the cattle diseases into the herd.

Yellowstone National Park's bison are infected with brucellosis too. Unlike tuberculosis, brucellosis is harmless to bison. In cattle, however, it causes cows to abort their calves. American authorities have repeatedly slaughtered bison that wandered out of the park toward cattle herds, triggering controversy. Ironically, analysis has shown that whenever brucellosis shows up in the area's cattle it's from elk, not bison.

Where the Banff and Blackfeet bison are concerned, at any rate, Alberta ranchers have little to fear. Both herds originated from Elk Island National Park, where rigorous disease testing and herd health measures have been in place for almost a century, partly in response to the Wood Buffalo disaster. Bill Hunt says Elk Island bison are the gold standard for conservation herds: genetically pure and disease free. "It can't get any better in terms of where those bison came from. They've been maintaining a disease-free status for decades."

If bringing bison back to even a small part of their original Alberta ranges is proving complicated and controversial, why even bother?

Retired park warden Wes Olson spent decades working with bison, first in Elk Island and then as the "buffalo cowboy" who coordinated the successful 2005 reintroduction of plains bison to Saskatchewan's Grasslands National Park. "Bison are a keystone species," he says. "They affect every other species that lives there."

One example: in areas with bison, almost a third of all bird nests are lined with bison hair, the second-warmest natural insulating material in North America. The hair not only increases egg hatching rates, it then protects nestlings from predators by masking odours. The absence of bison may help explain why many native grassland bird populations are in trouble.

Another example: bison dung supports over 300 native invertebrate species – a lost food resource for birds like sage grouse, which are now critically endangered in Alberta. Cattle droppings, on the other hand, support few bugs because most cattle are medicated with ivermectin and other chemicals toxic to invertebrates.

Bringing back bison may help bring back not only bugs and birds but frogs too. The big hollows worn into prairie by wallowing bison fill up each spring with snowmelt and rainwater. Toads, frogs and insects breed in those temporary wetlands. Restoring that critical habitat may help recover at-risk amphibian populations.

"Albertans are able to coexist with elk," says bison rancher Cody Spencer. "There are issues, but we know how to manage them. Why would bison be any different?" Pointing to the fact that farmers and ranchers already share land with wild bison in central Saskatchewan and eastern Utah, he says a study south of the border offers good evidence that agricultural conflicts may be less than feared.

In Utah's Henry Mountains, about 300 wild bison

share the range with domestic cattle. When areas where their cows congregate began to show signs of chronic overgrazing, ranchers suspected the bison were to blame. Researchers decided to monitor animal distribution and measure grazing rates using fenced enclosures. They found that the bison consumed barely 14 per cent of the available grass, mostly in areas where cattle seldom go. Jackrabbits, surprisingly, were the culprits – eating more than a third of the available cattle forage.

Spencer suggests that bison could even enable us to re-think the whole range agriculture industry. "It's awfully costly trying to force-fit cattle into our ecosystems," he says. "There are all the costs associated with calving, pesticide application, winter feeding, predator conflicts. You don't have those costs with bison."

Wild bison ranging freely in the Alberta foothills and prairies will create new opportunities – certainly for those who opt to hunt their own meat, but possibly even for ranchers interested in shifting from babysitting cattle to harvesting semi-wild bison. Regardless of how we exploit the recovered herds, though, a keystone species will once again shape ecosystems that have been without it for a century and a half. The changes may prove profound.

No less profound will be the impact on Alberta's Indigenous cultures. "What would happen if you took the cross away from Christianity?" asks Blackfoot Elder and teacher Leroy Little Bear. "The buffalo was one of those things. The belief system, the songs, the stories, the ceremonies are still there, but the buffalo is not seen daily…. The younger generation do not see buffalo out there, so it's out of sight, out of mind."

Little Bear played a pivotal role in drafting the Northern Tribes Buffalo Treaty, which led in part to the Blackfeet bison reintroduction. Initial signatories in the fall of 2014 included the Siksika, Piikani, Kainai and Tsuu T'ina First Nations, as well as Assiniboine, Gros Ventre, Sioux, Salish and Kootenai tribes from south of the Medicine Line. The Stoney Nakoda and Samson Cree First Nations signed on the following year. It was the first treaty among Indigenous nations in over 150 years.

"The Buffalo Treaty is historic," says Little Bear. "A treaty among just Indigenous cultures to work together on common issues: conservation, culture, education, environment issues, economics and health research. In the centre of that is the buffalo."

"Our elders said, we want to restore the buffalo. But it's a big job. We can't do it on our own. We need partners."

Marie-Eve Marchand is one of those partners. She was a founding member of Bison Belong, an advocacy network that sprang into life in 2009 to pressure Parks Canada to follow through on its commitment to bring bison back to Banff National Park and to build public support for the initiative. That work successfully completed, Marchand now provides administrative support and media coordination for the Buffalo Treaty.

"We eliminated the beaver and the bison, both keystone species," she says. "Now we are turning that around."

Marchand likes to cite Chief Ernest Wesley of the Stoney Nakoda, who said at one treaty discussion that the bison is important on many levels. "Think of it as our Walmart," he told her. "But think of it also as our Church."

"With the return of the buffalo," Leroy Little Bear adds, "those things that were part of those regularly occurring patterns in nature, the buffalo was part of it. So we're bringing back those regularities, and those regularities are part of what anchor our societies."

"But there's a whole lot more. There's also their larger role in the ecosystem. As a human species, we play a very small role in that ecosystem. And it's a big job to bring about an eco-balance. So we need help and the buffalo will do that. Is Alberta ready for that? Probably not."

Probably not. But if wild bison really are coming back to the western foothills and southern prairies, a lot of things will change – likely for the better. If we think of bison recovery as part of Alberta's reconciliation with First Nations, it might change us too.

6

WILD MEAT

HUNTING SEASON

Very early this morning, headlights crept down rural roads across Alberta, turned into the edges of fields and woodlands and blinked out. Had you been there, you might have heard the muffled closing of doors, low voices and the metallic sound of rifles and shotguns closing.

Had you been, instead, farther west, where mountains carve black silhouettes against the pre-dawn sky, you might have smelled wood smoke and seen shadowed figures moving against the flickering flames of campfires. The same low voices, the same metallic sounds; the fire doused suddenly with coffee dregs and creek water, and then stillness.

Aldo Leopold, universally acclaimed as the father of North American wildlife management, wrote in his classic 1949 work *A Sand County Almanac*: "Getting up too early is a vice habitual in horned owls, stars, geese and freight trains. Some hunters acquire it from geese, and some coffee pots from hunters."

Each autumn, hunters all across Alberta get up too early and set off into the dawn's first shadows in search of their prey – geese, grouse, deer, bighorn sheep, moose or pheasants. We've been doing it for millennia. That we still do it today, however, is a subject of recurring controversy. Agriculture long ago supplanted the need for most people to hunt their food, after all, and hunting by definition involves the killing of creatures. Ending a life is a profound act; why would one do it by choice? Why not just buy a pork chop?

Mary Zeiss Stange, for many years a professor and director of religious studies at New York's Skidmore College and co-owner of Crazy Woman Bison Ranch in eastern Montana, is one of many hunters who has debated whether hunting is an anachronism in our modern culture of placeless consumerism. In her contribution to an online compendium on "Does Hunting Make Us Human?" Stange asserts that, regardless of how you answer that question, "it is hunting that marks us human animals as predators – kindred spirits to the cougar and wolf, the grizzly and great horned owl. That we do, indeed must, meditate on the implications of our predation also distinguishes us (at least as far as we know) from those other nonhuman hunters. We human hunters have both the capacity and the responsibility to reflect upon the impact of our actions – our very existence – on the world about us."

And we do. It's impossible to spend hours afield, cut off from contrivance and distractions, immersed in everything that is real and vital about the living world that sustains us, without reflecting on the choices we make as hunters.

One of those choices is to take personal responsibility for the inevitable deaths that provide us with the meat we eat. Wild animals enjoy freedom, health and the ability to interact with one another and with their natural habitats right up until the moment they fall to a bullet or arrow. Death is no less final for them than for a cow, hog or chicken, but there can be little doubt that their lives are immeasurably richer. Consumers of domestic meat can ignore the messy question of how that meat found its way to the table. Hunters cannot dodge the question.

There is a way to avoid the question, of course: don't eat meat. But that simply changes the frame for what remains an ethical dilemma: things always die so that we may eat. If we choose to eat only legumes, grains and other plant products, then we cannot escape the truth that most of these are grown in monocultural fields. Entire ecosystems are destroyed to produce our vegetable foods. Voles, gophers, ground squirrels and mice are killed directly to keep them from eating those crops, and indirectly each time a field is plowed. If the argument against hunting is an argument against death, then it is essentially an argument against life. Things die so that other things might live.

So some of us hunt; there remains the question of how we hunt. Hunting reveals one's ethical values in a way that few other activities do. Every decision – whether to walk or to use a habitat-damaging off-highway vehicle; whether to respect our prey enough to ensure it a clean, painless death or to risk wounding with shots at distant or running prey; whether to give animals a better than fair chance of escape or to overwhelm their defences with space-age technologies – every decision a hunter makes is ultimately an ethical one. Or should be.

University of Alberta philosophy professor, Nathan Kowalsky, says that when he told a friend he was editing a book on hunting and philosophy, he got this response: "Lots of people think the combination is almost an oxymoron; philosophers don't hunt and hunters don't think."

True; some hunters don't. They're the ones who should stay home this fall.

FORGET DIETING

Checkout counter magazines and helpful Facebook friends continually offer advice on how to stop ailing and start looking and feeling good. But nothing seems to help. Obesity is rampant. Heart disease and cancer are major killers. It seems strange that health should be such a challenge when there is so little mystery to it. If you want to improve the quality of your life and delay your date with the Grim Reaper as long as possible, every doctor will tell you the same thing: eat well and exercise regularly.

Evidently, good advice isn't enough. Contemporary consumer culture seems to outfox our best intentions. Rather than throwing ourselves into diets and exercise programs only to face defeat a week or two later when we default to old habits, perhaps we would get farther by developing different habits of mind. How we think has a lot to do with how we act.

One of the habits of mind that seems to serve me well is to try to be personally acquainted with everything I eat, before I eat it. My wife and I grow a large vegetable garden each year. I hunt wild game for our meat. Each fall we visit favourite saskatoon, huckleberry and raspberry patches to gather fruit. We make jelly from crabapples rather than buy jam from the store. We know a lot of our food personally.

The benefits of taking responsibility for one's own food go to both sides of the health equation: diet and exercise.

Grocery store food has usually been mass-produced. Mass production relies on heavy applications of pesticides, petroleum, preservatives and processing. By the time those food products arrive on the table their good looks conceal a complicated chemical history. A lot of those chemicals end up inside of us, where they were never meant to be.

Besides, when food becomes a consumer product, we become a target for marketing. Food companies know how to use human biology to tempt us into buying their products: just add sugar, salt or fats – or all three. Our species has become biologically preconditioned by thousands of years of natural selection to fall for those three temptations. Lots of corporations are glad to help us overdose on them in exchange for our dollars.

The carrots, beets, potatoes, lettuce and tomatoes that Gail and I harvest each summer from our garden are chemical free. When we sit down to a meal from the garden, we know that we're eating the products of photosynthesis, not of mass production. If our backs and arms ache a little, that's our muscles thanking us for exercising them in the garden.

Or the hills. Last November I spent two weeks hunting elk in southwestern Alberta. Each morning I'd climb a ridge where I could glass the surrounding landscape in hopes of spotting a herd before their daily retreat to some dark forested refuge. When I spotted elk in the distance, I'd try to stalk to within shooting range. If the morning hunt came up empty, I would wander the woods until late afternoon, then climb another hill and watch until dark for elk to re-emerge in the open.

When hunting season ended, I had an unfilled elk tag. The bull elk I could have shot were all too far from the road to retrieve them safely and unspoiled. Fortunately, a friend who got an elk while hunting with me shared the meat. Now, when my wife and I sit down to steaks or burgers, I remember the animal that provided that meat. I know it lived wild, healthy and free until the moment it died – nobody crammed it into a cage, force-fed it steroids and antibiotics or herded it into a noisy abattoir before it became our food.

I also know I lost more than five kilograms pursuing the

elk I didn't get and helping to pull out the one my friend did. My lungs, heart and legs were strong by season's end. I had experienced a dozen sunrises and sunsets, visits with chickadees and squirrels, a bear encounter, wind in aspens, the scent of fallen leaves and the hard sting of wind-driven pellet snow. I had felt as free and wild as a wolf. That's a good feeling – but one that's simply not available in a grocery store.

Taking responsibility for hunting and gathering our own food has given Gail and me a far healthier diet than the supermarket could provide us with – although, of course, some of our food still comes from there. It's also given us more healthful exercise than we'd have gotten if we'd left others to do the work for us. Perhaps no less important, tending a garden or searching for wild meat are stress-reducing, soul-renewing sources of mental health too.

Perhaps the key to better health is not so much to worry about one's diet or to try to exercise more. It may be as simple as going out and getting one's own food.

CRAZED DEER

Bad news, Bambi: mad deer disease is here.

Chronic wasting disease (CWD) is the official name for our latest wildlife plague. CWD is not spread by bacteria or viruses but by deformed proteins. Like other prion diseases such as mad cow disease and scrapie, CWD always results in death from deterioration of the brain and nervous system.

Prion diseases don't jump from one species to the other. At least, that's what government agencies insisted when mad cow disease became epidemic in Britain in the 1990s. Then a not-so-funny thing happened: 140 human beings died from a fatal dementia they developed after eating beef from infected cows.

We may well be repeating that mistake with CWD. If so, Albertans who eat venison should be worried, because the disease is spreading across our province.

Since first appearing in captive deer and elk in Colorado, CWD has spread through parts of North America because of a public policy disaster – the decision to allow captive farming of native deer and elk. Actively promoted by state and provincial governments, including our own, game farming was seen as a way to diversify agriculture.

But native animals haven't had centuries of captive breeding to help them build tolerances to diseases perpetuated when animals are kept crowded together, sharing the same feed troughs and water tanks. And trucking infected animals from one crowded facility to another over long distances is a surefire way to spread diseases.

That's how CWD came to Canada – in an infected elk shipped to a Saskatchewan game farm from one in South Dakota. From that first infected Canadian game farm the disease spread to several others. Inevitably it soon appeared in wild deer near those farms.

In 2005 an Alberta hunter killed our first brain-wasted deer. It was far from being the last.

The earliest cases were along the Saskatchewan border south of Lloydminster. Infected deer are now being found along the Battle and South Saskatchewan rivers, the Red Deer River and, as of 2013, the Milk River. The disease is gradually spreading west toward Calgary and Edmonton.

Hunters can contribute deer heads to a government monitoring program. Out of 47,000 heads submitted by hunters for testing since the program started a decade ago, 164 turned out to be infected. Biologists found another 47 when wildlife officers culled large numbers of deer in key areas.

That's a low infection rate, but it appears to be increasing. CWD showed up in about 1.4 per cent of mule deer tested in 2012, but that increased to almost 2 per cent in 2013. Mule deer bucks have the highest rate of CWD infection, and doe whitetails have the lowest. Although it has been found in at least one Alberta moose, so far the testing results suggest that mule deer are its biggest victims.

The Alberta government continues actively to subsidize and promote game farming even though the industry has proven economically marginal. That awkward policy conflict may help account for why the government's hunting website assures hunters that "there is no evidence that CWD infects livestock or humans."

The World Health Organization (WHO) has no conflict of interest. Its advice is unequivocal: "All products from animals known to be infected with any prion disease (including BSE in cattle, scrapie in sheep, and CWD in deer and elk) should be excluded from the human food chain."

The Alberta government's public backgrounder on the public health risks involving CWD appears carefully crafted, in light of the tragic lessons from Britain's mad cow deaths, with an eye to future lawsuits: "Alberta accepts the current advice from local and international public health officials that there is no known health concern associated with CWD; however, persons should not knowingly consume meat of animals known to be infected with the disease."

In other words, we want to think it's safe – but don't eat it.

Government advice makes no reference to deer antler velvet or urine – two products sold by game farms – even though researchers have found that infectious prions concentrate in growing antlers and that body liquids, including urine, play an important role in spreading the disease. All over Alberta, some hunters douse their boots and hunting stands with "doe urine" purchased at hunting stores, in the hope of attracting a big buck. That urine comes from game farms. Hunters may unknowingly be contributing to the spread of their biggest nightmare.

Some of those same hunters are working against a solution too. The hunter-based Wild Sheep Foundation and some local fish and game clubs quietly subsidize trappers to kill off wolves. Wolves are coursing predators; they are on the job 12 months of the year looking for vulnerable prey. CWD turns deer into just the kind of prey that wolves are quick to find and kill. Dead wolves, however, can't kill sick deer.

The earlier a CWD-infected animal dies, the fewer prions it spreads. But hunter prejudice virtually guarantees wolves won't help clean up our growing mad deer disaster. Instead, the Alberta government hopes hunters will do it – the same hunters the government, reluctantly, advises not to eat infected animals.

This has not been Alberta's best example of intelligent wildlife policy.

QUIET, PLEASE!

Each November I hunt elk. In the eerie darkness I set out into a silent world, hoping to spot elk feeding at first light. After that first hour or two, the animals retreat into dense cover to bed down and listen for approaching predators.

A soft-footed cougar might have a chance of getting close to a resting elk, but not a clumsy human. Even when seemingly relaxed, their ears are always moving. A single snap of a twig will put them on full alert. One more cue, and they explode into flight, seeking a more peaceful retreat.

A quiet world is natural for elk and most other wildlife. It isn't silent out there, of course – wind, distant creeks and the soft voices of birds are threads softly woven into a stillness that has always pervaded the lives of wild animals and birds. When an unfamiliar noise invades that stillness, it demands attention.

Homo sapiens has been around for about 200,000 years. For 197,000 of those years, our ears were attuned to the same natural stillness as other species. It's only since the Industrial Revolution that our human world has become a noisy one. That's when we started using machines and putting fossil fuels to work running them.

When we escape back into nature, for whatever reason, we return to a natural stillness that is, in fact, our healthiest and original home. It's soothing to be away from massed noise. It's stressful to return to it.

The same applies for other species. Nathan Kleist, a University of Colorado researcher, measured stress levels in bluebirds and flycatchers nesting at various distances from natural gas compressors. Those compressors, as anyone knows who lives near one, generate a constant industrial drone. Kleist and his co-researchers found that birds nesting closest to the noisy compressors had stress hormone levels consistent with what is found in post-traumatic stress disorder (PTSD) sufferers. When experimentally subjected to a loud, sudden noise, nestlings near the compressors had much more dramatic increases in stress hormones and took longer to return to baseline levels than those in quieter nests farther away.

Rob Guralnick, an associate curator at the Florida Museum of Natural History, was one of Kleist's co-authors. In a summary report he says, "These birds can't escape this noise. It … completely screws up their ability to get cues from the environment. They're perpetually stressed because they can't figure out what's going on. Just as constant stress tends to degrade many aspects of a person's health, this ultimately has a whole cascade of effects on their physiological health and fitness."

Researchers have found that few songbirds nest near noisy freeways because they can't make themselves heard. Owls, which rely on hearing to zero in on prey, hunt less successfully where it's noisy. Species whose whole evolutionary history unfolded in a naturally quiet world simply can't cope with our hubbub.

Noise can even drive species to the edge of extinction. The sage grouse – once a hunted game bird – is now critically endangered in Alberta. Its natural habitat – the sagebrush country south of Highway 1 – is riddled with oil and gas infrastructure. Grouse avoid otherwise good habitat because it no longer offers the quiet they need.

Jessica Blickley of the University of California–Davis studied male sage grouse on the leks where they perform courtship dances each spring. Rather than risk disturbing the endangered birds, she chose to measure stress hormone levels in their droppings. Grouse exposed to industrial noise had almost 20 per cent higher corticosteroid levels than those using quiet leks. Blickley concluded that "chronic noise pollution can cause greater sage grouse to avoid otherwise suitable habitat, and can cause elevated stress levels in the birds who remain in noisy areas."

Historically, Alberta governments have never let endangered species hinder oil and gas development. That's why, in February 2014, the federal Department of the Environment finally stepped in. It issued an emergency habitat protection order prohibiting any new noise-producing industrial installations on 1672 km^2 of southern Alberta and Saskatchewan sage grouse habitat. That order was Canada's first recognition that natural quiet is a nature conservation issue.

If it's a nature conservation issue, then it's a human one too. For all our toys, indulgences and distractions, we are still part of nature. That's one reason my annual escape to the natural stillness of elk country is so important to me. Watching the dawn's first light spread slowly across a landscape so still it seems to be holding its breath is more than a hunter's moment of suspense. It's a return to the world that made us, to the stillness that lives at the heart of all existence – to the quiet that keeps us and our fellow creatures safe and sane.

CHARLIE RUSSELL'S GRIZZLY COUNTRY

I knew about ranching back in the 1980s. Ranchers were the bad guys who killed off bears and whose cattle trashed their habitat. Like most environmentalists of the day, I got my insights from urban-based environmental groups. In Alberta's ranch country the story seemed almost always to be about conflict between ranchers and carnivores, or conservationists and ranchers.

Then I met a soft-spoken rancher named Charlie Russell from the southwestern corner of Alberta who loved both bears and cattle ranching. He showed me how wrong I was.

To the extent that the story about ranching, bears and conservation is no longer framed by conflict, a lot of the credit goes to Charlie. He died in Calgary on May 7, 2018, predeceased by his parents, his son Anthony and a younger brother, John. In his final year, plagued by chronic health problems, Charlie told me he felt he hadn't done enough – that his messages about bears and bear country weren't getting through.

Typically, he had underestimated himself. "He was excited about bear country expanding," says his brother Gordon. "Grizzlies are going off the Eastern Slopes onto the prairies, onto the grain fields and farms. Much to the consternation of some of the landowners, but not all of them, fortunately. That was partly because Charlie was pretty successful."

"Man," Gordon adds, "the number of people who contacted us after he died and the things they wrote…. I don't think anyone quite grasped the impact that he'd had on people's lives."

Charlie was born in 1941 in the lee of the Rocky Mountains, the second child of Andy and Kay Russell. The province into which he was born had fewer people than live in today's Calgary.

In that Alberta, prosperity was still just a dream. Its cities were small and dusty, with few buildings exceeding three storeys. Most roads were gravel. Many of the young men were overseas, fighting a war. Oil had arrived – in fact, the Turner Valley oilfield reached peak production in 1942 – but it would be another five years before the Leduc #2 well blew in, ushering in an era of prosperity and urban expansion. Alberta's economy was still based on the uncertain fortunes of rural agriculture.

The first year of Charlie's life brought major flooding to southern Alberta, and that summer brought dust storms. Nature – with its floods, fires, storms and predators – was widely perceived as an adversary. Young men might be fighting fascism in Europe, but at home their families continued a decades-long fight against nature that seemed the only way to assure their future. Many ranchers still managed livestock in ways that made losses to predators inevitable.

Those losses were one reason why grizzly bear hunting regulations were so draconian. There was simply no room for grizzlies around people.

How bad was it for the bears? A 1947 government report, issued when Charlie would have been 6 years old, stated: "Grizzly Bear is still considered to be a predatory animal in some parts of the Province. In the areas lying to the south of the Crow's Nest–Medicine Hat branch of the Canadian Pacific Railway, Grizzly Bear may be shot at any time and without a license, the reason being that this area is mainly a farming and livestock area and the year-round open season is necessary for the protection of livestock. In addition ... the department employs special hunters to kill any Grizzly Bear in the Forest Reserves and the Waterton-Carbondale Game Preserves."

Grizzly bears didn't live on ranches when Charlie was young; they died there. Even so, he grew up to defend both bears and ranching in a world that undervalued each. His success is why "grizzly country" now includes western Alberta's agricultural landscapes and not just the remote mountain wilderness. Lately, grizzlies have even been seen in Calgary's urban fringe and farm country south of Lethbridge – unimaginable in Charlie's youth.

Charlie's mother Kay was the daughter of Waterton-area outfitter Bert Riggall. His father was legendary conservationist Andy Russell. Andy had hired on with Riggall as a wrangler and guide. In 1941 he wasn't famous yet; he was just a tall, rangy outdoorsman who had married the boss's daughter. When Riggall retired in 1946, Andy and Kay took over the outfitting business.

With his brothers, Dick, John and Gordon, and sister Anne, Charlie grew up among horses, wind and spectacular wilderness. The family lived in Waterton Lakes National Park during his younger years, and later on a ranch just north of the park. They rode deep into the mountains of southwestern Alberta and southeastern BC with pack trains, hobnobbed with tourists on day rides in the park and grew up as part of rural Alberta's cowboy culture.

The wilderness backcountry still held a few grizzly bears, animals Charlie had been told were dangerous and unpredictable. But the bears he met didn't seem scary. Mostly they just minded their own business.

By 1960, when his parents finally shut down the outfitting business because oil and coal roads were ruining the wilderness their clients sought, Charlie was in his late teens. With his older brother Dick he joined Andy on a new venture: filming wild grizzly bears in their natural haunts. The project had a dual purpose. On the one hand his father hoped to replace the family's lost outfitting income with another way of cashing in on their wilderness knowledge. On the other hand, it was a more idealistic venture: educating an increasingly urban society about the real nature of grizzlies.

The project started poorly. Bears were hard to find and too often fled before the Russells could collect any film footage. Andy later reflected that the turning point – and a big learning experience for all of them – came in 1962 and 1963 when the team headed north to Alaska's Denali

National Park. Park authorities wouldn't let them carry firearms. Without guns, they had to assume a more humble and respectful demeanour. And the bears appeared to respond, becoming more relaxed around them. The resulting movie, *Grizzly Country*, and Andy's subsequent book of the same name, amazed audiences who were expecting gory tales of bear attacks and depredations. Andy Russell showed them intelligent, patient animals more interested in eating roots than chasing people.

Charlie's views soon became even more radical than his father's; his encounters with bears led him to wonder if, rather than being more tolerant of people than commonly believed, they might actually like us. Charlie returned to Denali in 1964 and spent a summer alone among the bears with a 35mm camera. It was the beginning of a lifelong love affair. By the time I met him many years later, it was pretty clear that Charlie understood and liked bears better than he did most people.

"I had an experience with an incredible, beautiful bear that did something that puzzled me at the time and I wanted to explore it more," he told me during a 1996 interview. "She walked slowly up a ridge and at first I didn't think she even saw me because she was coming towards me but I moved around a bit and she'd definitely seen me.

I sat and talked to her and she came right up and lay down a few feet from me and she was obviously really interested in me.

"A few days later I saw her again and she did a similar thing only this time she lay down only ten feet from me, and in a totally relaxed, friendly manner....

"It was that experience that made me decide that there was something about these animals that wasn't generally recognized. When I got to ranching for a long period of time, about 18 years, I was determined ... to give them the benefit of the doubt and see if we could get along better."

After his experience in Denali, Charlie needed to make some money, so he found work with mining companies, first in BC and then in New Zealand.

"About that time," says Gordon, "Dad started making noises about selling the place. Charlie was the only one of us four guys that was willing to take it on. So he came back from New Zealand and ... bought the seven quarters from Mom. Belton Copps had bought the Cloudy Ridge Ranch and the two of them decided to put the two operations into one. They ended up with one of the biggest ranch operations in the area."

Charlie believed passionately that cattle ranching and conservation were meant to be the same thing, and that bears could live among cattle without conflict. His ranching experience proved him right. In all the years his family owned their ranch, they say they never suffered a single loss of an animal to a bear. Charlie told me about watching a grizzly work its way through a resting herd almost as if it were trying not to disturb the cows.

"It was a huge male and he would pick the widest path between animals, but some places that was only a few feet, and these cows would just lie there unless he came within 3 or 4 feet. I tried to carefully repeat this with my horse and quite a few animals got up from my horse and myself trying to do the same route. It pointed out to me that these animals must have been getting along very well all summer, even though I'd seen him eat a dead cow that I knew had died by itself."

Charlie was winding his ranch down and starting to work full time with bears when I went to Waterton in 1991 as the national park's conservation biologist. Our friendship had an awkward start. Charlie was mad at Parks Canada – my employer. He had good reason to be.

Waterton Lakes National Park gained recognition in 1979 as a UNESCO Biosphere Reserve under the United

Nations' Man and the Biosphere program. Biosphere reserves are meant to be global examples of how to integrate humans and the natural environment successfully. They normally include a core protected area – in this case, Waterton – and a surrounding zone of cooperation where economic land uses are managed in ways that sustain the area's natural values.

In Charlie's view, it was a perfect fit. The large ranches bordering the national park had protected natural habitats for decades. Large carnivores might be unpopular there but they, along with other native wildlife, still occupied the lightly peopled ranch lands. Charlie's vision was that, under the biosphere reserve concept, visitors to the area might not actually know where private land ended and protected park began. He volunteered to chair the new Waterton Biosphere Association and convinced some of his neighbours to participate too.

The 1970s and 1980s were a time of growing environmental awareness, but environmentalism, largely an urban phenomenon, was too often characterized by fault finding and finger pointing. Rural people were often seen as the bad guys, especially with regard to carnivores. Parks good; ranching bad. For its part, the ranching community was deeply offended by the environmentalist attacks, given that land stewardship was, for most of them, a core value.

In stepping up for the biosphere reserve Charlie was helping, consciously or not, to build a new paradigm. The Waterton Biosphere Association pulled rural people, urban environmentalists and Parks Canada together in common cause and mutual respect. Charlie's leadership got them talking with each other about shared values.

But Parks Canada is a bureaucracy and bureaucrats are often rule-bound. One of Parks Canada's rules was that major contracts should go to the lowest bidder. That's what Charlie was mad about when I met him in 1991.

Parks Canada needed a gravel supply for a major road project. Rather than protect the Biosphere Reserve's zone of cooperation, park bureaucrats accepted the lowest bid from an acreage owner who promptly bulldozed a large hill right beside the park entrance. The massive gravel pit destroyed native fescue grassland and replaced it with an ugly scar still visible to this day.

After assuring his neighbours that their good stewardship would be valued as something complementary, rather than in opposition, to the park's protection mandate, Charlie Russell felt deeply betrayed. The seamless transition the ranchers had bought into had been compromised by Parks Canada's decision to save a few dollars rather than buy responsibly sourced gravel. Charlie quit the Waterton Biosphere Association in disgust.

That experience deepened his view that only those with lasting roots in a place could be trusted to care for it sustainably. With the late Francis Gardner, Norm Simmons and other like-minded foothills ranchers, Charlie turned his back on bureaucrats and came up with a new idea for protecting bear country and the ranching industry that keeps it undeveloped: a land trust.

Francis Gardner once described the big ranches along southern Alberta's foothills as "working wilderness." Cattle might sometimes graze the grassland too hard or foul the creeks, but because that land supported the economy through ranching it was protected from logging, real estate development and other more destructive uses. That's why bears, elk, deer, trout and other wildlife like it there.

But the big ranches are under increasing threat. The price of cows continues to drop relative to the costs of fuel, equipment and other inputs. Aging ranchers don't always have family willing to take on the hard work required to keep things together. Real estate agents frequently come knocking on doors, hoping to turn ranches into residential acreages.

Charlie and his friends launched the Southern Alberta Land Trust Society (SALTS) to hold donated conservation easements on ranch lands – ensuring that those ranches remain undeveloped and undivided in perpetuity. It was the second land trust to operate in Alberta and the only one run by ranchers. The larger Nature Conservancy of Canada (NCC) is run mostly by business people. Many foothills ranchers didn't trust the NCC any more than Charlie trusted Parks Canada – they saw it as another bureaucracy of outsiders. That has changed over time; both land trusts frequently collaborate now.

Alan Gardner, a former executive director of SALTS, told me: "Charlie was part of getting SALTS started. He was committed to it and when Charlie said he was going to do something, he did it. He promised to donate conservation easements on his five quarter sections to SALTS. But the NCC went to Charlie and said 'If you put those five quarters with us, we'll give you $40,000 each.' Charlie turned it down. He said to me, 'I turned down $200,000. Sometimes I wonder if I should have done that but, you know, I'd already committed to SALTS.'"

"That was a lot of money back in 2002. But that's the kind of guy he was. His word was his bond."

Charlie certainly could have used the money. He had embarked on increasingly ambitious ventures to test his belief that bears and humans could get along peacefully. He even built his own ultralight airplanes to fly deep into bear country – crashing them more than once. His worst crash broke his back, but he hiked out for help anyway. Each time he got back in and flew back to his bears.

His passion for bears took him and then-partner Maureen Enns to Kamchatka, Russia, where he spent several summers in a remote area with one of the highest population densities of grizzlies on the planet. There he raised rescued bear cubs to maturity and helped them learn how to fend for themselves. He taught them to fish and forage, defended them from predatory adult male bears and even babysat the cubs of wild female bears who trusted him. His work there, and earlier in BC's Great Bear Rainforest, was chronicled in books and films that earned him a huge following among wildlife conservationists, animal rights groups and people from all walks of life.

Most see Charlie's legacy as changing how we think of

bears. "Everyone says that grizzly bears are dangerous and unpredictable," he told me. "Well they aren't. They can be dangerous but usually that's because we treated them badly. And they aren't unpredictable at all. We're the ones who are dangerous and unpredictable. The bears just want to get along."

But Charlie's lesser-known legacy was no less important: building bridges among rural Alberta ranchers and environmentalists to ensure that bear country – not the remote wildernesses of rock and ice to which bears were relegated when Charlie was a boy, but the lush, well-vegetated ranches and farmlands of western Alberta – will always be there. SALTS has more than 23,000 acres under conservation easement. The NCC has protected almost 140,000 acres of Alberta's foothills under easements or by outright purchase.

And bears are welcome there. Ironically, given that he quit it in disgust, that's partly due to the Waterton Biosphere Association that Charlie helped get up and running. Inspired by Charlie's work, the WBA's Carnivores and Communities Program now helps ranchers and farmers coexist with bears safely. Under the leadership of Cardston-area rancher Jeff Bectell, they pioneered the use of "deadstock" bins – bear-proof metal containers for livestock that die during the spring calving season. Instead of getting bears in trouble, carcasses now get recycled as compost. The WBA helps ranchers replace leaky feed sheds with bear-proof storage bins, enclose beehives with electric fences and learn how to use bear spray to keep themselves safe.

It's a different world than Charlie was born into. In some ways it's a better one, because he showed us that knowledge, respect and even friendship are possible between humans and bears – not the fear and loathing perpetuated by frontier-era stories.

Charlie also helped change our stories about ranching. In doing so he helped to ensure that, in spite of the massive waves of landscape change that swept North America in recent decades, the grizzly country of Alberta's western foothills remains largely intact, sustained by ranch families whose stewardship values and personal ethics Charlie Russell both honoured and exemplified.

7

BEING BETTER

KILL THAT CAMERA

The little boy leaned over the stone barrier, staring at a herd of bighorn sheep. The rest of his world, clearly, had vanished; he was in the moment, watching animals he had probably never seen before, filling himself with a new awareness of their scent, their strange eyes, the scratching sound of their hooves ....

"Cody, look over here!"

His mother was in position, smartphone at the ready. The little fellow turned slowly, as if emerging from a dream, saw the phone, and was instantly transfigured. He threw back his head, smeared a big grin across his face and pointed back at the sheep.

Click. Another family memory captured and ready for sharing on social media. "Look at Cody; isn't he cute in front of those animals?"

And just like that, a camera killed the magic in another encounter with the real world. A boy was reminded that the world might hold other creatures but it's really about him. He's the star; they're stage props.

That's how we raise a lot of kids these days. And that's how we're conditioning ourselves. The ubiquity of the camera now that we all live permanently attached to a cellphone or tablet means our lives are increasingly digitized rather than experienced. We no longer observe; we click. And then we forget and move on in search of the next opportunity to create an image we hope will convince others, and ourselves, that our lives are vivid and delightful.

If I see one more picture of someone jumping in the air, throwing up their arms in feigned delight in front of some iconic landscape I'll ... I'll ... I'll crush my camera with an axe. Or maybe not. Like everyone else, I fear, I'm addicted to that nefarious killer of honest connection with the real world.

Brain scientists tell us that the mind responds to repeated behaviours by hard-wiring the neural pathways that support them. Repeat an action or a thought frequently enough, and that part of the brain begins to reinforce itself, similar to how repeated use strengthens a muscle. From the first time a photographer teased an image out of a lens and onto paper, society has worked to make photography as widely available and inexpensive as possible. Today we all do it, and we all do it a lot. In doing so, we train our minds to see the world not as a place of meaning and mystery but as a series of images.

Worse, we train our minds to see ourselves as the centre of all those images.

Columnist Zoe Williams, writing in *The Guardian*, says: "It has become routine for celebrities to broadcast banal information and fill Instagram with the 'moments' that constitute their day, the tacit principle being that once you are important enough, nothing is mundane. This delusion then spills out to the non-celebrity; recording mundane events becomes proof of your importance."

Between the cameras that travel everywhere with us and social media that enables us to share imagery, we are rewiring our brains. Constant clicking – especially selfies – shuts down the parts that look, ponder and reflect on the real world, instead shifting neural activity to the narcissistic task of creating posters of ourselves.

A few weeks after my disturbing observation of the little boy and the bighorns, my wife and I got trapped in a bear jam. A grizzly was gorging himself on berries at the edge of the forest. As we waited, a man jumped out of an suv and, phone in hand, hurried down into the ditch. At the edge of the timber he turned his back on the bear and clicked some selfies.

Fortunately, the bear was busy and, probably, used to idiots. The man did not die an ugly death in front of his family. I doubt he even properly saw that bear until he uploaded his precious photo onto Facebook. He clearly saw it not as a real being – merely a chance for a cool photo.

At least that bear had a life. Earlier this year a petition to rescue a polar bear from the Grandview Mall Aquarium in Guangzhou, China, garnered more than 285,000 signatures. The bear is held in a small glass enclosure in a busy mall. Hundreds of people rap on the glass each day in hopes of getting it to stand for their selfies; it has nowhere to hide.

Like the Jasper bear jammer, those phone clickers aren't interested in bears; their interest is in themselves. They want to show themselves with a bear. Its suffering is irrelevant.

Thinking of giving someone a camera for Christmas? Do them – and everything else – a favour. Give them a pair of binoculars and a notebook instead. They don't need pictures. They sure don't need selfies. They need to learn to see, to ponder and to care about things other than themselves.

Clicking makes the world all about us. It isn't.

BURNING FOR FUN

Global crises used to be times when shared sacrifice took over from self-indulgence, bringing out the best in citizens and communities. During the Second World War, for instance, Canadians rationed sugar and chocolate to leave more for overseas troops. Government-imposed gas rationing forced families to do without camping holidays, but people took pride in knowing they were freeing up fuel for the military. People held metal drives to help build trucks, tanks and armaments. Citizens and governments were united in common cause and the certain knowledge that personal restraint mattered.

Between global conflicts, that sense of common purpose and self-sacrifice vanishes back into a sea of competing self-interests. When a new great war begins, it can take a while to reawaken a shared willingness to sacrifice for the greater good.

It's time; the next great crisis is here. Storm surges are devouring shorelines around the world. Extreme weather events have become the new normal. Weird winters, devastating floods, scary droughts and phenomenal storms fill the headlines. We argue over the possible impacts of atmospheric warming when they are already upon us. Another one degree of global warming? Unthinkable – but imminent.

Climate change is a far greater threat than any war. It is, in fact, the greatest war – a war for a livable planet. No cause has ever more urgently demanded government leadership and, among citizens, a willingness to sacrifice. Instead, however, we act like children in a sandbox, too absorbed with our toys to heed danger.

Our grownup toys are themselves part of the problem. Among the worst: off-highway vehicles that dump CO_2 into the atmosphere while damaging the vegetation and wetlands that would otherwise pull carbon out of the air and store it in soil and peat. According to Mike Berners-Lee's book *How Bad Are Bananas? The Carbon Footprint of Everything*, simply to manufacture and sell a motor vehicle produces about 360 kg of CO_2 for every thousand retail dollars. Albertans spend an estimated US$82.5 million annually to buy motorized off-highway vehicles – in other words, an annual CO_2 output of 29.7 million kg.

Assuming – conservatively – that only three-quarters

of the 118,000 off-road vehicles registered in Alberta are used for recreation, and assuming that the average user travels only about 500 km each year, those machines cover 44.25 million km annually. The average fuel efficiency of off-road vehicles in 2011 was 5.95 litres/100 km. So that's 2,632,875 litres of fuel burned each year – for fun. Burning a litre of gasoline, according to the US Environmental Protection Agency, produces 2.35 kg of CO_2. So Alberta's recreational off-road vehicles spew more than 6 million kg of CO_2 each year.

Combining the annual carbon footprint of building and selling new off-highway vehicles with the carbon footprint of operating them, we pour almost 35 million kg of CO_2 into the atmosphere each year simply to drive, rather than walk, on outdoor trails.

We should reduce frivolous CO_2 emissions during a global climate crisis. But there's another issue here too. Health researchers have proven that walking, especially in nature, is among the best ways to improve health. Healthcare costs are among the biggest line items in government budgets. De-carbonizing our economy will be particularly hard on Alberta government revenues; we need smart ways to cut costs. Improving public health would do that.

If people are too unconcerned about climate change to stop using carbon-spewing toys and to start walking again, then a truly enlightened government should heavily tax those toys. It's an approach that worked for reducing tobacco consumption. Some of the revenues could even be rebated to citizens who buy hiking boots instead. When people aren't prepared to make responsible choices during a global war for a livable planet, government needs to go beyond rhetoric and drive real change.

Alberta's government is continuing to encourage off-road vehicle users to play on our public lands. By letting those vehicles damage vegetation and soil that would otherwise pull carbon out of the air and sequester it underground, the government is actually breaking its own laws. The Public Lands Act makes it illegal for anyone – including government – to "cause, permit or suffer ... any act on public land that may injuriously affect watershed capacity ... [or] the creation of any condition on public land which is likely to cause soil erosion."

Our parents and grandparents once set aside self-indulgence for the common good. Facing a crisis greater than any war of man, their descendants continue to choose motorized play regardless of its climate and public health impacts. And rather than use tax policy to discourage such abuse, our government, in ignoring its own laws, chooses complicity.

STEWARDSHIP

My dad used to derive a quiet pleasure from driving his station wagon past stuck four-wheel-drives. Alberta's foothills and mountains had few good roads in the 1960s. Dad took things slow on our camping adventures. When the roads got slick, he got out and put chains on the back wheels. We kids would wave as we clanked slowly past young men whose overconfidence in their powerful machines had got them mired in the ditches.

Alberta's public lands seemed wild and pristine to us kids in those days. Campgrounds were clean, quiet and rarely crowded. Big logging companies hadn't arrived yet to denude the hills. Sometimes we saw deer, bears or lynx. Trout were abundant, at least for those willing to walk a bit. It was a great place to grow up.

We walked ourselves skinny every summer. Alberta's increasingly fevered search for black gold had oil companies carving seismic cutlines across hill and dale. Those cutlines offered shortcuts cross-country into creeks that had hitherto only been tantalizing squiggles on Dad's maps. Breaking out into a quiet meadow full of birdsong after two hours of hard hiking was always a magic moment. Who knew what monster fish might lurk here? And always, farther upstream, remote valleys hinted at more magic and mystery.

I was born into an Alberta composed mostly of quiet, conservative people. People like Dad who took things slowly and carefully – not just on slippery backroads but in life generally. People like Mom who preferred to give rather than take. The first time I heard an old rancher say that he wanted to be able to look back and know he'd left the land a bit better than when he found it, it made sense to me. That was what one expected to hear in an Alberta whose people considered stewardship a way of life, citizenship a duty and frugality and restraint basic virtues.

But things changed.

New oil wealth gave way to a sense of impatient entitlement among many who tasted the easy abundance of the oil-rich 1970s. Soon traditional Alberta virtues were passé. Well-being was no longer enough; prosperity became an overriding policy priority. The path to prosperity involved aggressive exploitation of our public lands. Forestry ramped up. Oil and gas ramped up. People could afford new toys like off-highway vehicles (OHVs), dirt bikes and snowmobiles, so recreation ramped up too. Both at work and at play, a more self-absorbed generation began filling once-peaceful hinterlands with damage and abuse.

The seismic lines had been left for nature to reclaim, but their new grass and shrubs vanished as expensive OHVs turned them into muddy raceways. Once-remote trout streams were no longer hidden rewards for those willing to walk a couple of hours – they were fished out and full of tire tracks. No mystery remained farther up-valley either; people and their motorized toys were there too.

As destructive pastimes scarred the landscape, new-comers came to see damaged land as normal. So they didn't even try to take care of it. They brought their beer and their guns and their stereos. The rest of us stopped going. Our own public lands neither felt safe for families nor offered quiet recreation in wild, clean countryside like they used to.

I suspect that most Albertans are still like that rancher who said he wanted to leave the land better than when he found it. But our public lands no longer reflect that stewardship ethic. Instead, they now bear the scars of a more recent ethos of selfish entitlement. It's like they ceased being ours.

Alberta's public land should be a living legacy for future generations – healthy forests and meadows yielding clean water in streams full of native trout, where families find peace, inspiration and healthy outdoor exercise, and where the best Alberta values are passed on from one generation to the next. Instead, our native trout are now classified as threatened species. Gullied landscapes spill muddy floods each spring; then streams run low and silty in summer. Those who see land and streams merely as challenges for motorized play have taken over. The rest of us have had to retreat to a few protected parks where quiet still prevails. But that simply overcrowds those parks.

Kids need green, living places where they can be introduced to healthy exercise, wild nature and the ethics of stewardship and restraint. Our public lands used to be those places. They could be again. That would require a government with the courage and vision finally to call an end to land abuse by a noisy minority and give our public lands back to all of us – to be enjoyed with the quiet decency that has always defined Albertans at our best.

BETTER CONTAGION

Earth is a mess. It's been 400,000 years since the planet's atmosphere last held this much carbon dioxide. And we keep pumping out more. The consequences – melting permafrost, increasingly frequent and violent storms, eroding coastlines and crop failures resulting from erratic weather – are everywhere.

Insect populations – essential to life – are in rapid decline. German researchers report that even protected nature reserves have barely a fifth as many flying insects as they had half a century ago. Once-common birds such as the barn swallow (down by 70 per cent) and meadowlark (down by more than half) are in trouble. A 2019 report by the North American Bird Conservation Initiative shows that Canada has lost half of our shorebird, grassland bird and aerial insectivore populations. Birds that depend on native prairie are down by as much as 90 per cent – several are classified as endangered.

These are only some indicators of a global environmental

catastrophe for which we humans are to blame. If, as some religious traditions assert, humanity is called to be stewards of the Creator's riches, it's time we were fired for dereliction of duty and incompetence.

A lot of people feel hopeless. How can any one of us hope to turn the tide on such massive, inexorable problems? If those problems are systemic, then surely the only solutions are big ones that exceed our individual reach – such as population control, a transition away from capitalism and hydrocarbon fuels or wholesale conversions of an unconcerned populace to new ways of being.

Actually, no. There are real things we can do at the personal level that could make a real difference. Big changes have almost always started at the individual level. When enough individuals have shown change to be needed, possible and achievable, then that change becomes contagious and unstoppable.

Problems arise one decision at a time. Solutions do too. One would need a pretty huge ego to believe that one, single-handedly, could save the world. But saving one's home place? Maybe. And that's, after all, the scale we live at.

So what would be most useful for individuals to do at that scale? Here are some ideas:

Make the switch to locally sourced, sustainably raised

and ethical food. The Alberta farm families who produce it often struggle to stay in business because most of us are too lazy or cheap to buy food that wasn't produced on factory farms or distant lands. Raising food without added chemicals, without abusing animals and without damaging the land and waters costs more for farmers, so it's going to cost more for us too. If we want to change our relationship with nature, the first step is to change our relationship with food. We won't change agriculture for the better unless we're prepared to start putting our money where our mouths are.

As a consumer, ask hard questions when you shop. Refuse overpackaging, disposable junk and the exploitation of staff and suppliers. Hold capitalism accountable. If you don't do it, who will?

Tear out your lawn. Start a garden. Maybe start a community garden. Lawns are ecologically and culturally dead spaces that waste massive amounts of water, fuel and chemicals. Gardens, on the other hand, are living places. They yield food, attract birds and insects and can help build community too. One at a time, we could make lawns socially unacceptable and healthy homegrown food normal again. That would be good.

If you really need a car, switch to a hybrid or electric vehicle next time you replace your wheels. Buying a low-carbon vehicle not only helps reduce your impact but also sends a market message both to other consumers and to industry. Don't buy another vehicle that runs solely on gasoline ever again.

Get up the courage to ask your MLA for a meeting. Ask them to promote policies that protect natural habitats, rivers, wildlife and family farms. Publicly acknowledge their leadership when they do. Politics don't need to be partisan, but politics are important. Those who profit by exploiting nature are good at doing politics; the rest of us need to be even better at it.

Raise outdoors kids. Get off the couch, turn off the cellphone and take them hiking, fishing, hunting or paddling. Nature time strengthens family bonds, makes kids physically healthy and helps them fall in love with nature. People who love nature are motivated to care for it. Think of it as succession planning, because your kids will continue your efforts – or lack of effort.

This world is literally staring ecological disaster in the face. But our job is not to save the world. That's too big for any one of us. Our best work may be simply to change how we live in our home places, and to help those changes catch on.

The best solution for a sick world is to be a healthy germ, and to spread better kinds of contagion.

OUR BEST STORIES

Henry Stelfox arrived in Alberta during one of the worst winters in our history – the endless cold of 1906/07 that, by some estimates, killed more than half the cattle in the province. He and his wife eventually settled near Rocky Mountain House and raised nine kids. He ranched cattle, cut wood, dabbled in real estate and bought furs as they adapted to the challenge of making a living in a young and not particularly prosperous province.

Farther south, that same killing winter set events in motion that helped Aubrey Cartwright start up his D Ranch on Pekisko Creek. Disheartened by their losses, some of the small homesteaders in the area decided to sell out. Cartwright and his partner consolidated some of those small holdings into a large ranch. His son Jim eventually passed it on to Gordon and John Cartwright.

"I remember as a young boy asking my father how much land we owned," Gordon Cartwright said recently. "My father took care to explain, that no man could truly own land; the deed or lease by which we held the land was really our covenant to look after it."

The Cartwrights looked after it well. Faced with the prospect of a major gas field development in their green, well-watered landscape, the Cartwright brothers joined their neighbours in a costly but ultimately successful effort to head it off. They then arranged for their leased pasturelands to be included in a new, protected Heritage Rangeland. On his deeded land, Gordon locked in his family's tradition of responsible stewardship by registering a conservation easement with the Southern Alberta Land Trust Society. The easement ensures the land can never be broken or subdivided.

Henry Stelfox created a conservation legacy too – not least by passing on his stewardship ethic to grandkids devoted to forest conservation, landscape health, wildlife and fisheries. Stelfox believed in public service as a duty, not as a sinecure. He signed on as the region's game warden and travelled the upper Clearwater River country keeping an eye on wildlife conditions and making sure hunters and anglers stuck to the rules. His work brought him into contact with Cree, Chippewa and Stoney people who lived in those remote foothills, and he soon became their advocate to Edmonton and Ottawa.

When the government insisted that Stelfox accept

payment for his services, he quit. It was against his principles to accept money for serving the public interest – an interesting contrast to the expense account and severance scandals we hear about too often these days. He continued to write about and promote conservation and played a key role in organizing the Alberta Fish and Game Association – turning hunters and anglers into a force for conservation rather than exploitation.

On the Blood (Kainai) Reserve near Cardston, Api'soomaahka (William Singer) has taken on the daunting task of restoring diverse native prairie to land his father cultivated decades ago. Working with Kansie Fox and other members of his tribe, Singer is trying to bring back medicine plants lost to the plow. Even some of their names have been lost, but he is working with tribal Elders to find new Blackfoot names as they bring their home place and their culture back to vigour. "I'm not here to make money off the land. I'm here to heal it," he said in an interview with Stephanie Wood of *The Narwhal*.

The Cartwrights and Stelfoxes, with Singer, Fox and countless others, are the stuff of which Alberta was made: principled, caring people who choose stewardship over greed, giving themselves to Alberta rather than taking more than the land and waters can spare.

Aritha Van Herk popularized the idea that Alberta's culture is defined by its mavericks – larger-than-life risk takers who grabbed our sprawling natural landscapes and shook fortunes out of them. It's an attractive creation myth for those who see resource exploitation as a way to accumulate wealth; as such, it's been widely misappropriated to support a vision of this place founded on greed and ambition. Farther afield, Alberta's seen as a land of defiant rednecks in pickup trucks. Visit the foothills on a May long weekend, and that stereotype might not seem far from the mark. At least until the latest downturn in oil and gas prices, anyone could come here from away and become an instant "Albertan" with a pickup truck, a monster home, a ball cap and a case of beer.

But that version of Alberta leaves out the Stelfoxes and Cartwrights whose quiet work and self-sacrifice not only built our province but preserve much of it from the reckless exploitation that continues to make it less than it was meant to be. It omits conservationists like Kerry Wood and Grant MacEwan who gave us a very different set of stories about what Alberta is and who Albertans are. Lois Hole and Jean Lougheed, champions of the arts, built heritage and philanthropy, don't contribute much to the greed-based story of Alberta – but they, too, are among the real Albertans who define us at our best. The quiet labours of Indigenous people like Kansie Fox and Api'soomaahka, who work to restore their lands and cultures from the ravages of colonialism, go ignored when a province lets itself be defined by tales of pillage and privilege. This place we love has never lacked for people who love it back; we just don't give them enough air time.

"In the Beginning, there was the Word," it says in the Book of Genesis. Who controls the word, controls the story – and a culture is the product of stories. As Alberta struggles once again to shape a sustainable future in the face of yet another bust in the oil patch, it might be well to revisit the stories by which we define ourselves.

Wild Rose Country's best stories – Alberta's true genesis stories – don't derive from exploitation; they come from the kind of deep commitment to our home place that expresses itself in caring stewardship of its lands, water, fish, wildlife and communities. We have lots of those stories. And we have it in us to make a great many more.

SELECTED BIBLIOGRAPHY

Alberta Biodiversity Monitoring Institute (ABMI). 2017. *The Status of Human Footprint in Alberta*. https://abmi.ca/home/reports/2018/human-footprint.

Alberta Climate Change Office. 2015. *Climate Leadership Plan: Implementation Plan 2018–19*. Edmonton: Government of Alberta.

Alberta Department of Lands and Mines. 1947. *Annual Report of the Department of Lands and Mines of the Province of Alberta for the Fiscal Year Ended March 31st 1947*. Edmonton: Government of Alberta.

Alberta Energy. 2017. *Coal and Mineral Development in Alberta: 2017 Year in Review*. Edmonton: Government of Alberta.

Alberta Energy. 2018. *Coal and Mineral Development in Alberta: 2018 Year in Review*. Edmonton: Government of Alberta.

Alberta Energy. undated. "About Coal." https://www.alberta.ca/about-coal-overview.aspx.

Alberta Environment. 2003. *Water for Life: Alberta's Strategy for Sustainability*. Edmonton: Government of Alberta.

Alberta Environment and Parks. 2018. *Castle Management Plan*. Edmonton: Government of Alberta.

Alberta Environment and Sustainable Resource Development. 2013. *Alberta Wetland Policy*. Edmonton: Government of Alberta.

Alberta Land Institute. 2017. *Economic Evaluation of Farmland Conversion and Fragmentation in Alberta*. Edmonton: University of Alberta.

AMEC. 2009. *South Saskatchewan River Basin in Alberta: Water Supply Study*. Lethbridge: Alberta Agriculture and Rural Development.

Antweiler, Werner. 2015. "Coal Mining and Selenium." *Werner's Blog*. Sauder School of Business, University of British Columbia. https://wernerantweiler.ca/blog.php?item=2015-02-07.

Barker, A.A., J.T.F. Riddell, S.R. Slattery, L.D. Andriashek, H. Moktan, S. Wallace, S. Lyster, G. Jean, G.F. Huff, S.A. Stewart and T.G. Lemay. 2011. *Edmonton–Calgary Corridor Groundwater Atlas*. Edmonton: Energy Resources Conservation Board, ERCB/AGS Information Series 140.

Beaubien, E.G., and M. Hall-Beyer. 2003. "Plant Phenology in Western Canada: Trends and Links to the View From Space." *Environmental Monitoring and Assessment* 88, no. 1: 419–29.

Berners-Lee, Mike. 2011. *How Bad Are Bananas? The Carbon Footprint of Everything*. Vancouver: Greystone Books.

Berry, Thomas. 2006. *The Dream of the Earth*. Berkeley: Counterpoint. (Originally published 1988).

Blickley, J.L., K.R. Word, A.H. Krakauer, J.L. Phillips, S.N. Sells, C.C. Taff et al. 2012. "Experimental Chronic Noise Is Related to Elevated Fecal Corticosteroid Metabolites in Lekking Male Greater Sage-Grouse (*Centrocercus urophasianus*)." *PLoS ONE* 7, no. 11: e50462. https://doi.org/10.1371/journal.pone.0050462.

Bremer, Eric. 2009. *Potential of Rangelands to Sequester Carbon in Alberta*. Research Paper. Alberta Sustainable Resource Development, Lands Division.

Campbell, Robin. 2018. "Canadian Coal Driving Global Growth." *Canadian Mining Journal*. https://www.canadianminingjournal.com/features/canadian-coal-driving-global-growth/.

Cantafio, Leanne, and Cathryn Ryan. 2014. "Quantifying Baseflow and Water-Quality Impacts from a Gravel-Dominated Alluvial Aquifer in an Urban Reach of a Large Canadian River." *Hydrogeology Journal* 22: 957–70.

Carson, Rachel. 1962. *Silent Spring*. Boston: Houghton Mifflin.

Casey, A. 2010. "The South Saskatchewan River Runs Dry." *Canadian Geographic*, October 1. https://www.canadiangeographic.ca/article/south-saskatchewan-river-runs-dry.

COSEWIC. 2017. *Assessment and Status Report on the Burrowing Owl* (Athene cunicularia) *in Canada*. Ottawa: Committee on the Status of Endangered Wildlife in Canada.

Cox, Wendell, and Hugh Pavletich. 2020. "16th Annual Demographia International Housing Affordability Survey." *Demographia* report. http://www.demographia.com/dhi.pdf.

Daschuk, James. 2013. *Clearing the Plains: Disease, Politics of Starvation, and the Loss of Aboriginal Life*. Regina: University of Regina Press.

Douglas, Howard. 1904. *Report of the Rocky Mountains Park of Canada for the Year Ended June 30, 1903*. Ottawa: Department of the Interior.

Ducks Unlimited Canada. undated. "Wetland Loss." http://www.wetlandsalberta.ca/wetland-loss/.

Farr, D., A. Braid and S. Slater. 2018. *Linear Disturbances in the Livingstone-Porcupine Hills of Alberta: Review of Potential Ecological Responses*. Edmonton: Government of Alberta, Department of Environment and Parks.

Gadd, Ben. 2005. "Fighting Frankenmine: A Naturalist's Lament." *Alberta Views*, July 1. https://albertaviews.ca/fighting-frankenmine/.

George, Tharun. 2018. "Montem Resources Raising $20 million to Develop Metallurgical Coal Mines in Canada." *Proactive Investors Australia*.

Government of Alberta. 2020. Public Lands Act, RSA 2000, c. P-40.

Government of Alberta. undated. "Chronic Wasting Disease – Public health." https://www.alberta.ca/chronic-wasting-disease-public -health.aspx.

Government of Canada. 1998. Parks Canada Agency Act, SC 1998, c. 31. https://laws-lois.justice.gc.ca/eng/acts/P-0.4/.

Government of Canada. 2000. Canada National Parks Act, SC 2000, c. 32. https://laws-lois.justice.gc.ca/eng/acts/n-14.01/.

Government of Canada. 2013. Emergency Order for the Protection of the Greater Sage-Grouse. SOR/2013-202.

Hauer, Richard, and Erin Sexton. 2013. *Transboundary Flathead River: Water Quality and Aquatic Life Use*. Glacier National Park: Rocky Mountains Cooperative Ecosystems Study Unit.

Hebert, Rachel. 2017. *Ranching Women in Southern Alberta*. Calgary: University of Calgary Press.

Holroyd, G., and K. Van Tighem. 1982. *The Ecological (Biophysical) Land Classification of Banff and Jasper National Parks, Volume III: The Wildlife Inventory*. Edmonton: Canadian Wildlife Service.

Huntington, Henry, Shari Fox, Fikret Berkes and Igor Krupnik. 2005. "The Changing Arctic: Indigenous Perspectives." In ACIA (ed.), *Arctic Climate Impact Assessment* (pp. 61–98). Cambridge: Cambridge University Press.

Huntsinger, L., and N.F. Sayre. 2007. "Introduction: The Working Landscapes Special Issue." *Rangeland* 29, no. 3: 3–4.

Hurley, Adèle. 2015. "Let's Make Groundwater an Issue of National Security." *Globe and Mail*, December 4.

Jaremko, Deborah. 2020. *Understanding Inactive and Orphan Wells in Alberta*. Canadian Energy Centre. https://www.canadianenergycentre.ca/understanding-inactive-and-orphan-wells-in-alberta/.

Kleist, Nathan J., Robert P. Guralnick, Alexander Cruz, Christopher A. Lowry and Clinton D. Francis. 2018. "Chronic Anthropogenic Noise Disrupts Glucocorticoid Signaling and has Multiple Effects on Fitness in an Avian Community." *Proceedings of the National Academy of Sciences of the USA* 115, no. 4: E648–E657. https://www.pnas.org/content/115/4/E648.

Lee, Peter. 2004. *Boreal Canada: State of the Ecosystem, State of Industry, Emerging Issues, and Projections*. Global Forest Watch, Report to the National Round Table on the Environment and the Economy, Edmonton.

Leopold, Aldo. 1966. *A Sand County Almanac, with Essays on Conservation from Round River*. Toronto: Random House (*A Sand County Almanac* originally published 1949; *Round River* originally published 1953).

Madsen, Becca, and Hannah Kett. 2011. "What Part of 'No Net Loss' Does Alberta Not Understand?" *Environmental Marketplace*. https://www.ecosystemmarketplace.com/articles/what-part-of-no-net-loss-does-alberta-not-understand/.

Matthews, Evan. 2017. "Simpcw Chief Responds to Backlash after Hunt in Jasper National Park." *Jasper Fitzhugh*, October 12. https://www.fitzhugh.ca/simpcw-chief-responds-to-backlash-after-hunt-in-jasper-national-park/.

Morgan, Jeffrey. 2019. "Alberta Ranchers, Farmers Furious over Oil and Gas Companies' Failure to Clean Up their Geriatric Wells." *Financial Post*, December 18. https://financialpost.com/commodities/energy/alberta-ranchers-farmers-furious-over-oil-and-gas-companies-failure-to-clean-up-their-geriatric-wells.

NASA. 2020. "Carbon Dioxide." In *Global Climate Change: Vital Signs of the Planet.* August. https://climate.nasa.gov/vital-signs/carbon-dioxide/.

North American Bird Conservation Initiative Canada. 2019. *The State of Canada's Birds, 2019*. Ottawa: Environment and Climate Change Canada. www.stateofcanadasbirds.org.

North Saskatchewan Watershed Alliance. 2009. *North Saskatchewan River Basin: Overview of Groundwater Conditions, Issues, and Challenges.* Edmonton: Worley Parsons, Infrastructure and Environment.

Ogilvie, Sheilagh. 1979. *The Park Buffalo.* Calgary–Banff Chapter, National and Provincial Parks Association of Canada.

Perez-Valdivia, Cesar. 2009. *Groundwater in the Canadian Prairies: Trends and Long-term Variability.* Master's thesis, University of Regina.

Peterson, Rachel, and Nigel Sizer. 2014. "Tar Sands Threaten World's Largest Boreal Forest." *World Resources Institute Blog.* July 15. https://www.wri.org/blog/2014/07/tar-sands-threaten-world-s-largest-boreal-forest.

Pomeroy, John. 2014. Personal communications.

Ranglack, Dustin, Susan Durham and Johan du Toit. 2015. "Competition on the Range: Science vs. Perception in a Bison–Cattle Conflict in the Western USA." *Journal of Applied Ecology* 52, no. 2: 467–74.

Rodney, William. 1996. *Kootenai Brown: Canada's Unknown Frontiersman.* Surrey, BC: Heritage House.

Rosenberg International Forum on Water Policy. 2007. *Report on Water Policy to the Ministry of Environment, Province of Alberta.* https://ucanr.edu/sites/rosenbergforum/files/310852.pdf.

Rosenberg, Kenneth V., Adriaan M. Dokter, P.J. Blancher, J.R. Sauer, A.C. Smith, P.A. Smith, J.C. Stanton, A. Panjabi, L. Helft, M. Parr and P.P. Marra. 2019. "Decline of the North American Avifauna." *Science* 366, no. 6461: 120–24.

Russell, Andy. 1967. *Grizzly Country.* New York: Alfred A. Knopf.

Russell, Charlie. 2017. *Spirit Bear: Encounters with the White Bear of the Western Rainforest.* Toronto: House of Anansi.

Russell, Charlie, and Maureen Enns. 2002. *Grizzly Heart: Living Without Fear Among the Brown Bears of Kamchatka.* Toronto: Random House Canada.

Saha, Purbita. 2017. "How Cattle Ranchers Are Helping to Save Western Grasslands and Birds." *Audubon Magazine,* Spring. https://www.audubon.org/magazine/spring-2017/how-cattle -ranchers-are-helping-save-western.

Salten, Felix. 1928. *Bambi: A Life in The Woods.* New York: Simon and Schuster.

Sanchez-Bayo, F. 2018. "Systemic Insecticides and Their Environmental

Repercussions." In Dominick A. Dellasala and Michael I. Goldstein (eds.), *Encyclopedia of the Anthropocene* (pp. 111–17). Oxford, UK: Elsevier.

Saher, Merwan. 2015. "Environment and Parks—Systems to Manage Grazing Leases." In *Report of the Auditor General of Alberta*, July 2015. https://www.oag.ab.ca/reports/environment-and-parks-systems-manage-grazing-leases-july-2015/.

Shanker, Deena. 2019. "The Hottest Thing in Food Is Made of Peas, Soy, and Mung Beans." *Bloomberg Business Week*, August 21. https://www.bloomberg.com/news/features/2019-08-21/fake-meat-is-hot-led-by-impossible-foods-and-beyond-meat.

Smith, Robert. 2018. "Don't Eat Meat! Save Yourself and Humanity." *Wall Street International Magazine*, October 24. https://wsimag.com/food-and-wine/44393-dont-eat-meat.

Smith, W., and R. Cheng. 2016. *Canada's Intact Forest Landscapes, Updated to 2013*. Ottawa: Global Forest Watch.

Special Areas Board. 2006. *Special Areas Board Response to Environmental Issues Identified from Completed Public Consultation Forms*. Special Areas Water Supply Project report.

Stange, Mary Zeiss. 2014. "Hunting the Edges." *Does Hunting Make Us Human? Blog*, March 3. Center for Humans and Nature.

Stegner, Wallace. 1969. *The Sound of Mountain Water*. New York: Doubleday.

Stelfox, Henry. 1972. *Rambling Thoughts of a Wandering Fellow, 1903–1968*. Edited by John G. Stelfox. Self-published.

Stephenson, Amanda. 2018. "Firm Pushes for $700M Coal Mine in Crowsnest Pass." *Calgary Herald*, August 18.

UNESCO. 2017. *State of Conservation: Wood Buffalo National Park (Canada)*. https://whc.unesco.org/en/soc/3615.

US Environmental Protection Agency. 2013. *Methodologies for U.S. Greenhouse Gas Emissions Projections: Non-CO_2 and Non-Energy CO_2 Sources*. https://unfccc.int/files/national_reports/biennial_reports_and_iar/submitted_biennial_reports/application/pdf/methodologies_for_u_s__greenhouse_gas_emissions_projections.pdf.

Van Herk, Aritha. 2002. *Mavericks: An Incorrigible History of Alberta*. Toronto: Penguin Canada.

Wood, Stephanie. 2020. "Meet the People Saving Canada's Native Grasslands." *The Narwhal*, July 31. https://thenarwhal.ca/carbon-cache-grasslands/.

NOTES

1   Update: In 2020 the United Conservative Party government surprised Albertans with an announcement that it was rescinding the
Alberta Coal Policy. They had consulted with nobody, not even the
First Nations whose treaty rights were affected. The change was at
the request of coal industry lobbyists.

The Alberta Coal Policy was developed in the 1970s by the
Progressive Conservative government of Peter Lougheed after six
years of planning and extensive public consultation. Based on an
evaluation of where the province's strategically important resources are found and where those resources overlap, the Coal Policy
identified areas where coal mining was encouraged and other areas
where it was restricted or prohibited.

The Front Ranges of the Rocky Mountains were mostly in Zone
2: an area too important for prairie water supplies, outdoor recreation and fish and wildlife to allow strip mining. That protection
is now gone. Mining speculators, mostly from Australia, have already leased most of the newly available land and have bulldozed
new roads and trenches to delineate the coal resources they hope
to develop.

The Grassy Mountain mine is no longer the only, or even the
most important, strip mining threat facing our headwaters. Zone

2 covers almost 1.5 million hectares of wild country along the Rockies, from near Waterton to Grande Cache.

2 Update: Even before a spike in bankruptcies spawned by the 2020 pandemic, the *Financial Post*, in late 2019, had reported that the Orphan Well Association was now contending with nearly 3,500 orphaned wells and a potential liability of 93,805 additional inactive wells. At least 15,000 wells drilled before the mid-1960s had not yet been remediated. By 2020, as investors fled Alberta's oil patch, the abandoned well problem had exploded.

In response to the dire economic situation, the federal Liberal government transferred $1.2 billion to Alberta to help accelerate well remediation. Alberta's UCP government loaned the Orphan Well Association an additional $100 million. Alberta may soon employ more workers to clean up old wells (mostly with borrowed public money) than actually to produce conventional oil and gas.

3 Update: Anger at the loss of motorized recreation opportunities in the new Castle parks helped mobilize a reactionary movement that replaced the NDP with a far right United Conservative government in 2018. The UCP promptly set to work undoing the progressive initiatives of their predecessors. Minister of Environment and Parks Jason Nixon appointed a new advisory group with a specific mandate to advise on how to restore motorized recreation opportunities in the Castle parks. The long siege of the Castle, unfortunately, has been renewed.

LAND ACKNOWLEDGEMENT

We would like to also take this opportunity to acknowledge the traditional territories upon which we live and work. In Calgary, Alberta, we acknowledge the Niitsítapi (Blackfoot) and the people of the Treaty 7 region in Southern Alberta, which includes the Siksika, the Piikuni, the Kainai, the Tsuut'ina, and the Stoney Nakoda First Nations, including Chiniki, Bearpaw, and Wesley First Nations. The City of Calgary is also home to Métis Nation of Alberta, Region III. In Victoria, British Columbia, we acknowledge the traditional territories of the Lkwungen (Esquimalt and Songhees), Malahat, Pacheedaht, Scia'new, T'Sou-ke, and W̱SÁNEĆ (Pauquachin, Tsartlip, Tsawout, Tseycum) peoples.

❦

KEVIN VAN TIGHEM, a former superintendent of Banff National Park, has written more than 200 articles, stories, and essays on conservation and wildlife which have garnered him many awards, including Western Magazine Awards, Outdoor Writers of Canada book and magazine awards, and the Journey Award for Fiction. He is the author of *Bears Without Fear*; *The Homeward Wolf*; *Heart Waters: Sources of the Bow River*; and *Our Place: Changing the Nature of Alberta*. He lives with his wife, Gail, in Canmore, Alberta.